My Life, My Illness, and My Assurance in God

To Scott,
Blessings to you.

Pat

Phil 4:19

Patricia A. Miller

"The grass withers and the flowers fall, but the word of our God endures forever"
Isaiah 49:8 NIV.

My Life, My Illness, and My Assurance in God

Published through Lulu.com
Raleigh, North Carolina

ISBN – 978-1-365-10221-9

Printed in the United States of America

Published by lulu.com
Raleigh, NC

Acknowledgements:

Kylie Wells, Caryl Hackett, Julie DeJohn, and Damon Davis for help with the technical skills.

Lynn Towersey for staging materials.

Nancy Kortes for proofreading my book.

Tom Colburn for helping me self-publish.

Cover design by Misha Colburn.

Drawings by Patricia A. Miller.

Thanks to everyone.

Contents

Chapter 1

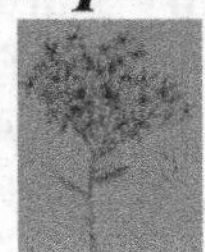

" A wise son makes a glad father, but a foolish son is a sorrow to his mother"
Proverbs 10:1 ESV.

My Parents and Grandparents

My mother, Virginia Thurber and her mother, Grandma Lena Nielsen were buying groceries at the general store in the little town of Langston in Montcalm County, Michigan when mom met my dad, Fred Hansen. She, being a beautiful young lady, was noticed by my dad who was working in the grocery store.

Soon after that, she went to a dance with a different young man at Clifford Lake. It was held in a dance hall built around a tree near the Clifford Lake Hotel. My father was also there at the dance hall. He loved to dance and was very good at it. At some point that night he asked mother to dance. She ended up being taken home by my father instead of the one who brought her.

Dance Hall around the tree

In a sense, my life really started at Clifford Lake. Later, I was to live at Clifford Lake for over fifty years.

My mother's father was Charles Thurber, Sr. who left my grandmother after mother was born. Mother was the youngest of the three children. My grandpa was what you might call a ladies' man. I believe he married another time or two. He rarely came to see his children.

Mother was raised on a farm owned by her step-dad, Odin Neilsen and her mother, Lena. When mother was young she had saved her money for flower seeds for the garden but she had problems raising her flowers. The chickens loved to scratch up the seeds. This probably was the beginning of her love for gardening.

She had two older brothers, Charles and Lawrence. One day when she was 14 years old, Lawrence, and his friend, Melvin Larsen went with her to West Lake near Langston for a swim. Melvin was struggling in the water. Lawrence went and tried to help him. Tragically, mother watched both of them drown. Mother ran to get help but it was too late to help either one of them.

In 1934, her brother, Charles, married the Larsen boy's sister, Lillian. They had two children, Joan and Gerald. They settled in Stanton and remained there for the rest of their lives. Charles was our milkman when they still delivered milk to our homes. He grew flowers and gladiolus. Joan was three years older and we remained close through the years. She was a favorite niece of my mother.

Mother went to high school in Lakeview. There were no buses in those days, so she worked for a couple of different families for her room and board in Lakeview. The first family where she lived, the father was a dentist. She would do their washing and ironing and make pies before she went to school in the morning. The second family was the Youngman family who then owned the funeral home. She helped take care of their children.

Dad's parents were both from Denmark. Grandpa John P. Hansen, arrived with his family when he was about six years old. Grandma, Sine Christiansen Hansen, came to America when she was around 23 years old. She had trouble speaking English because of coming to the US as an adult. They both probably came through Ellis Island in the 1800's. They had 11 children. Two died at a young age. Dad was the oldest of the boys. They were raised on a farm outside of Stanton on Musson Road. The early settlers of the Stanton area were predominantly of Scandinavian and German descent. Dad graduated from Stanton Rural Agricultural School. He worked in another grocery store in Stanton. Later he worked for a plumber and heating man which helped him to learn the trade. Eventually he became a Master Plumber. Grandpa was a tinsmith so they started a plumbing and heating business. Grandpa made all the furnace ductwork while Dad was the salesman. He installed and did all of the service work.

In 1936, there was a very bad snow storm. Blizzard followed blizzard, often accompanied by below-zero temperatures. Schools were closed, the trains couldn't get through and men had to shovel out some roads because the drifts were too deep for plows to handle. Many people in rural areas gave up on using their cars and resorted to horses and sleighs or traveled on foot. Mother and her parents lived on a dead end road that was about a half mile long. My dad walked in groceries for them. Grandma and grandpa always cared a lot for dad. Dad was a nice, quiet caring man.

Dad being five years older than mom, had already graduated from high school. Mother turned 18 early in her senior year at Lakeview. A week later, they decided to elope to Indiana to get married. You could get married in Indiana without your parent's permission. Mom still finished her senior year of high school and graduated in 1937.

Chapter 2

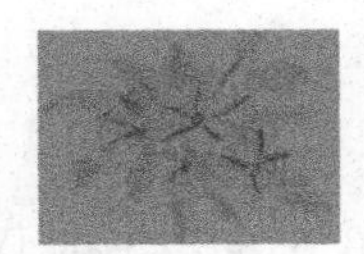

"And he has given us this command : Anyne who loves God must also love their brother and sister"
1 John 4:21 NIV.

My Early Life

One year later, I was born at home on Musson Road. Grandma and Grandpa Hansen lived across the road. I was born June 10, 1938 weighing 9 lbs. 4 oz., 21 inches long. A newspaper clipping said Aunt Lillian came and helped mother and me. In those days, you were supposed to stay in bed several days.

My baby picture

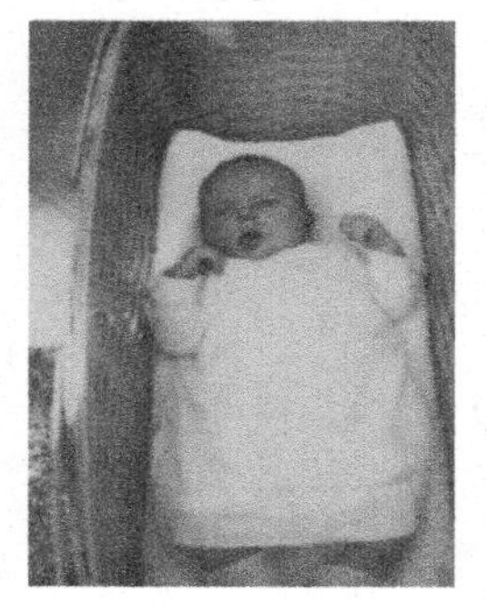

Me ready to pick flowers

My sister, Phyllis, was born when I was two and my brother, Lloyd, when I was almost four. They were born in our home in Stanton. I remember playing in the sandbox with my sister. In the summer, dad would clean a wooden fishing boat and put water in it so we could play in it. We had a dog named Jigs. You couldn't talk about going anywhere around Jigs because he would sit back by the backdoor and wouldn't move.

Grandpa and Grandma Neilsen, Me, Mom and Dad

When I was three, we went on a trip to Rhode Island. Grandma and Grandpa Neilsen went with us because Grandma was raised there. We visited Roger Williams Park. Roger Williams was the founder of Rhode Island. We visited Grandma's brother, David Biddle, and some cousins. I can still remember being in the backseat of the car with grandma and grandpa. We went across a long bridge and we were singing, "You are my sunshine." I never forgot that moment. I can still remember sitting in the backseat between them.

Grandma and Grandpa Hansen

One day, mother was leaving Grandma Hansen's with Phyllis and me. By this time, Grandma and Grandpa had moved from the farm on Musson Road and bought a house in Stanton on Lincoln Street. We got in the car. I was learning to pull the door shut on the car but I didn't have it quite shut. Mother went around the corner and I flew out. She ran in the ditch. Then Phyllis, still a baby, fell on the floor of the backseat. She was okay. Mom was able to drive out of the ditch and when we got home, Mom called the doctor to the house. I was okay, just scrapes and bruises.

At age 3, I was playing tunes on the toy piano. At age 4, mother contacted Edwin Petersen of Greenville to see if he would give me piano lessons. He said "No, I don't start anyone that young." Sometime later, my Grandma Neilsen saw his wife on the streets of Greenville. She would stop and start up a conversation with anyone. She said to Mrs. Petersen that her husband needed to come and listen to her granddaughter play the piano. By that time, mother and dad had purchased an old upright piano. Mr. Petersen did come and listen. He asked me if I knew the alphabet. I asked him, "frontwards or backwards?" He told me that part when I was an adult. He smiled and said "I could never get over that." So, I started taking piano lessons which went on until I graduated from high school.

On my fourth birthday, we went to Grandma and Grandpa Hansen's for dinner. Aunt Vernice and Aunt Sarah both graduated from Stanton High School that night. I remember Grandma making homemade bread. She had large bins in her cupboards for flour. Their family was large, so at holidays there was a large gathering of relatives at their house. Grandpa used to play the violin for us. He was known as "Fiddler John" and he played for dances and weddings. They had a pump organ at their home which I played after I learned to play the piano.

We would go and visit Grandma and Grandpa Nielsen on the farm. Grandma liked to set me on her lap, rock me, and sing the old hymn, "Rock of Ages". She could play her old upright piano a little, especially hymns.

A painting of the crooked bridge which was painted by Brenda Buchholz Smith

We usually went the shortest way to see Grandma and Grandpa Nielsen which was west of Stanton to Lake Road which went across *the crooked bridge* north of Hillis Rd. When we headed home, we would ask if we could go the way of the "singing bridge." This was a longer way home through Langston. The sound from the bridge was the metal ridges that the bridge was made of.

Chapter 3

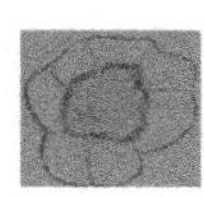

"Children, obey your parents in everything, for this pleases the Lord" - Colossians 3:20 NIV.

My Young School Years

The summer I turned five, we lived with Grandma and Grandpa Nielsen while our house in Stanton was being remodeled. Mom would help grandpa on the farm. She drove a Ford tractor for him. It was fun riding on the tractor. We used the outhouse to go to the bathroom. At night, we used a pot that sat inside the closet.

Grandma was a good cook. She cooked and baked on a woodstove for many years. I liked helping her in the kitchen, making bread and pies. She churned her own butter in a butter churn which was a wooden device that converted cream into butter.

It was a typical plunger-type. The chickens we ate were cleaned and we plucked the feathers from them on the big round kitchen table after grandpa caught them and removed their heads. I used to go and check on all the chickens to see where they laid their eggs in the chicken coop and different places in the barn. That was a lot of fun collecting eggs. I used to help grandpa in the barn and I learned to milk cows by hand.

On occasion, Grandpa would start his Model T by cranking it, then he'd take me when he went to get groceries in Greenville. We would always stop at the dairy in town and have a chocolate soda before returning home.

The visits from Grandpa Thurber were very few in number through the years. A picture was taken one time when he came with our cousins, Joan and Gerald. Phyllis looks like a little Shirley Temple, my brother, Lloyd doesn't look too happy.

Phyllis, Gerald Thurber, Grandpa Thurber, Me, Joan Thurber, and Lloyd.

That fall, I started kindergarten. My teacher was Lois Beal. Dad took me to school every day because he worked in Stanton. After school, I would sit on the bank of grass by the school and talk to my new friend, Marilyn Miller. Marilyn and I remained friends into adult life. Marilyn's dad was the local banker. Her mother stayed home raising kids. Marilyn had an older brother, Chuck, and a younger sister and brother, Ann and Kim.

I often stayed at Grandma and Grandpa Hansen's until it was time for dad to get out of work and we went back to the farm.

Some friends from school, neighbors and cousins attending my fifth birthday party.

My first grade teacher was again, Lois Beal. I remember liking her very much. She is over 100 years old and still a very nice and pleasant lady. Her memory was still good when I chatted with her around the time of her 100th birthday. We have communicated every year at Christmas time.

While living on Lincoln Street near the school, I took tap dancing lessons from Donna Williams who lived in the neighborhood. I remember learning the "buffalo step." I could do that step for many years when I tried it. I played the piano for her to teach other students taking tap dancing lessons.

When I was in the second grade, we moved from Lincoln Street in Stanton to downtown above Dad's plumbing and heating business.

When I was in the third grade, we were bused out to a country school named Hemmingway northwest of Stanton. That was a fun time.

My lunch pail with a little Dutch girl on it.

We could take our lunch pails outside to eat when the weather was nice. My dad made Phyllis and me a tin lunch pail. Our teacher, Veda Flynn, read the Laura Ingalls Wilder books to us. I remember the school had a pot belly wood stove that she stood by as she read to us. My girlfriend, Lorelei Anger, has a copy of a letter Laura Ingalls Wilder wrote to our class, because we all sent a letter to her.

One day in the month of May, we were going to go on a hike behind the school. We had to climb a fence with barbed wire on the top. I was the next to last to climb over. I caught my arm near the elbow on the barbed wire which tore my skin. I couldn't get loose so had to stand on my tippy toes. The girl behind me crossed over and ran for Mrs. Flynn. She came and had to lift me up so she could unhook me. She left the kids at the school and drove me to my mother. I had 3 stitches. Nowadays, I probably would have at least ten stitches. Mrs. Flynn was a wonderful teacher. She wrote in my autograph book, "Keep up the Good Work" all through life and remember, "Honesty is the Best Policy."

One summer, my parents rented a cottage on nearby Derby Lake in the Derby Gardens area. We rented it from Art Carothers, our next door neighbor when we lived on Lincoln Street in Stanton. One weekend, my Aunt Martha and Uncle Joe Jackson came to visit us at the cottage at the lake. Aunt Martha was Dad's sister. I think Dad and Uncle Joe went fishing. They didn't have children yet then. We would swim there. I remember the beach was very sandy on that side of the lake.

The cottage inspired them to purchase a place on the lake. So they bought 5 lots on the south side of Derby Lake. They had a basement built which we stayed in until they could build the house on it. We loved to swim. We spent long days in the water. We had a babysitter, Avis Cooper, while our parents went to work. Later, our cousin, Joan Thurber, babysat us.

My first fish.

I liked to go fishing just a short way out in front of our house. I usually caught perch. Dad taught me how to clean my own fish. We used to walk over to Derby Gardens store to buy candy or ice cream. When we got a little older, Dad put in a garden across the road so we could do some work. One summer, we grew pickles and sold them in Sidney. I made about $75 and bought my new school clothes. I also planted gladiolus bulbs, taking after Uncle Charles, who always planted a garden full of them to sell.

Besides enjoying fishing and swimming, I loved listening to the Detroit Tigers on the radio and playing Canasta. One day I had 2 hamburgers with large slices of onions. They tasted so good that day but the next day my stomach ached and I was vomiting. I thought it was the extra onions but the next morning I woke up with severe abdominal pain.

Mother drove to get the doctor and while she was gone, the pain became worse. By the time she and the doctor got there I was starting to get some relief. He said it was my appendix and I needed to go to the hospital. They said I needed to have surgery. I remember another doctor giving me anesthetic drops that somehow I inhaled and I went to sleep.

My appendix had ruptured. I was in the hospital 7-10 days. They gave me antibiotics. They didn't get you up very fast in those days. I was in the old Sheridan hospital which was an old large home.

Old Sheridan Hospital

Chapter 4

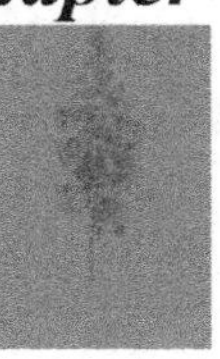

"Let him have all your worries and cares, for he is always thinking about you and watching everything that concerns you" - 1 Peter 5:7 TLB.

My Fun High School Years

One of the greatest things in my life is my girlfriends from my school days. In the fifth grade, a new student, Mary Lou Miel and I became very good friends. We remained friends for many years. Mary Lou's dad, Clif, was the shop teacher in high school. Her mother, Katheryn, became the hearing technician at the schools in later years. She had two younger sisters, Susie and Julie. When we were around 12, I remember walking in a field next to her Grandma and Grandpa Daoust's in Stanton. We decided to give our life to Jesus Christ. Later in life, I wasn't sure of my salvation and gave my life to him a couple of more times. I told Mary Lou about it and she said, "We already did that years ago, don't you remember?"

My friend Shirley Ewing lived a couple of blocks from me. Her parents owned the dry cleaners across from my parents' store downtown. She had a brother Gordie, my brother's age.

Another friend, Lorelei Rader, lived a few blocks north of us on Lincoln Street. Previously, her father, Harold, was president of Pleasant View Lutheran College at Ottawa, Illinois, and her mother was Dean of Women. That is where they met. They moved back to Lakeview, Michigan because his grandma who helped raise him was ill and needed care. He became Superintendent of Schools and they moved to Stanton. They had 3 other children, Gerald, Alayne, and Luke. Her father died when she was two. Her mother became a social worker to support her family. Lorelei's aunt, Lena Rader, graduated from Lakeview High School with my mother in 1937.

Lena married Fred Meijer who later built the very successful Meijer grocery store chain throughout the Midwest. He and his father started a store in Greenville and after that developed stores in Grand Rapids. No matter how successful they became, Fred and Lena never forgot their old friends.

Ardeth Porter also lived in town. Ardeth's mother was a school teacher and her father worked for the Road Commission. She had two older brothers, Lyle and David.

Christa Hansen also lived north of Lorelei on Lincoln Street. Christa's mother, Maxine, was a stay at home mom and her dad Dr. Carl, was a local physician and surgeon. She had an older brother, David, who died of leukemia in his late teens. Years later, they adopted a boy, Terry.

All of us girls stayed close. When we were 40, Mary Lou decided we should all get together for a trip and we decided to go to Chicago for a few days.

Ardeth, Mary Lou, Marilyn and Lorelei in Chicago.

Ardeth, Lorelei, Marilyn and Me.

We continued getting together every year after that in different places. We still see each other when we can. Shirley and Christa rarely make it now because Shirley and her husband, Gordon, live in Redding, CA. Christa lived most of her life in San Diego. She was a teacher and her mother lived near her in her later years.

I also took accordion lessons from Mr. Petersen for many years. I had a small 12 bass accordion, then later a 60 bass and the last one was 111 bass. The bellows are squeezed together to make the music sound. The left hand plays on the bass keys making the chord sound where the right hand plays the melody on the piano keys.

I played the accordion for community groups and a minstrel show in Greenville. Recently I played the accordion for church.

Playing the accordion at Greenville's Minstrel Show

I played in the high school band. I started on a trumpet which belonged to my parents' friend, Seymour Stebbins. Later, I played the alto horn and French horn which belonged to the school. In marching band, I played the bell lyre. We wore ties with our uniforms and I learned to tie my own tie. I was the student conductor when our band director, Mr. Currier was busy. My sister, Phyllis, was the head drum majorette. I sang in the high school choir and sang or played the piano in school musicals. I always played "Pomp and Circumstance" on the piano for seniors to march in many graduations.

During high school I went to Greenville to Mr. Petersen's home to take organ lessons. I practiced my organ lessons at the church and I played for many church services.

In my early high school days, my sister, Phyllis, her friends, Arlene Petersen and Judy Steele, and I started singing. We would sing and harmonize popular songs. We practiced at our home or at Arlene's house where her mother loved to hear us sing. We were known as the "Harmonettes". We entertained at Stanton's festival in the summer, called Stanton Anniversary Days. Our manager was Seymour Stebbins who owned and operated Stebbins Hardware. He did everything to promote us even making arrangements for us to have singing lessons. Our first song was "Side by Side." After a year or so, Judy didn't want to sing with us anymore but the three of us continued on singing every year at Stanton Anniversary Days.

We sang on Channel 8, WOOD-TV station, in Grand Rapids. We sang at fairs, festivals, charity events and for many organizations in and around Stanton. We tried out for the Lowell Showboat one year. We entered a competition in Big Rapids at the Mecosta County fairgrounds taking first place and won $50.

One time we sang at the Veterans' Home in Grand Rapids where Grandpa Thurber lived. I believe we sang there at his request. He was a veteran from World War 1, but he never left Michigan during the war.

He rarely came to see us when we were young just like he rarely came to see my mother or her brothers when they were children. When I was in high school, he wanted to live in Stanton near mother and Uncle Charles. He got an apartment in Stanton. Mother did his laundry but not much more. At some point, he started an interest in genealogy. He contacted Thurber's all over the United States. He used his money for stamps, stationery, index cards, etc. He discovered people we were related to, such as James Thurber, the famous humorist and cartoonist (See Epilogue).

In our junior year of high school, one of my classmates, Jerry Miller, asked me out. I had to turn him down because I already had a date that night with his cousin, Melvin Wittkopp, from Greenville. Not that I was popular and had lots of dates, it just happened that way, but Jerry didn't give up. The next week he asked me out again. We went to a track meet with my friend, Christa and her boyfriend, Lanny Perkins. We dated again the following night with my sister, Phyllis, and her boyfriend, Warren Wells. He kissed me goodnight for the first time. That began a long relationship for the rest of our junior year and all of our senior year.

Sometimes, I would go to church with him. He was the Superintendent of the Sunday School in his church on Fitzner Road. He had asked Jesus into his life years prior at the Langston Church.

I started going to Sunday School at the United Church in Stanton, probably when I was under 10 years of age. The United Church was the Congregational Church and the Methodist Church that had joined together. One summer, I went to Bible School there. The minister and another man, took me into an office. I believe they wanted me to accept Jesus as my Savior, and they wanted me to sign a paper. I didn't understand and it scared me and I didn't think I should sign anything.

In 1951, that church burned down. I lived a couple of blocks away, so I went and watched it burn. Dad was on the fire department, but I don't know if he helped with that fire or not. There was a group of Congregationalists trying to get the church back because they didn't like what was being taught there. After the fire, they won in court, so they got the land back. My folks joined that group and we went to Sunday School and church at the

Masonic Hall which was above the Fire Department. Marjorie Brake was the pianist and Marion Hunsicker played the violin. In 1952, the new church was built on that land on the corner of Camburn and Bradford Street where the old church had burned down. It was a beautiful new church. It has a large dramatic stained glass window depicting Christ in the sanctuary. Light filtering through the stained glass illumines the image of Christ and offers an inspirational focal point for worship.

Shirley Ewing and I would clean the church on Saturdays. The floors were all tile, upstairs and down and we often had to mop all of it. At noon, we would make our lunch and sit on a children's table with the sun shining in on us through the basement windows. We liked to make tuna fish sandwiches and cream of celery soup. To this day, I can't eat that soup without thinking about those days.

I formally joined the church when I was in high school. I sang in the choir. We had a choir director that I liked. Her young boys would come to practice with her and they were live wires running up and down the aisles. Later, our band director, Jay Currier, was the choir director. He was a perfectionist, but very good. We had a new Hammond organ at the church which I played when they needed a substitute. It was a challenge to play for him as he directed the choir.

Jerry and I having fun at Lake Michigan

The last year of high school was busy with studies, being on the yearbook staff, musical activities, and Jerry with his sports. He even tried basketball in his senior year. He was good at football and especially track.

For graduation, I directed our class singing a song and gave the salutatorian speech. We graduated on May 23, 1956.

Mom, Me and Dad

For our senior trip, we took a bus to Grand Rapids and got on a train for Chicago. We had lunch at the Palmer House Hotel in Chicago and then got on a boat that went on Lake Michigan and headed north. We stopped and spent a day at Mackinac Island. When we left there we headed down Lake Huron to Detroit. It got stormy and most of us got sick. We docked at Detroit and took the train back to Grand Rapids. We had lots of fun on the train. Going on this trip with your honey was great.

Jerry joined the naval reserves in high school and the summer after graduation, he went active duty into the Navy with his friend and classmate, Rex Engel. Jerry and Rex went to Great Lakes Training for their basics. They were separated then for the remainder of their two years of active duty. Rex was a gunner on a naval destroyer in the Pacific Ocean and later went to the Suez Canal when there was conflict in the Mediterranean Sea area. Jerry stayed at Great Lakes Training base and was in the fire department.

After a few months, he was transferred to Norfolk, Virginia and was assigned to a naval tanker, the US Truckee. The tankers fueled other ships. He traveled over the equator a few times to the Ascension Island in the South Atlantic Ocean about 1,000 miles from Africa.

Jerry 1957

Chapter 5

"Do unto others as you would have them do to you" - Luke 6:31 NIV.

Nursing School Days

My music teacher, Mr. Petersen wanted me to go to the Chicago School of Music. It would have been a four year program and was a big city that didn't sound good to me. I would have still been in music school when Jerry got out of the Navy. I had become interested in becoming a nurse. I had a friend from Ionia, Delores Cusack, who went into training the prior year. I read some of the Cherry Ames novels about nursing. I especially liked the one about becoming a student nurse. So I applied at Butterworth Hospital in Grand Rapids and was accepted into their nurses training program.

It was a three year program. When I went down for testing and interviews, Mom and I met Maureen Wood and her mother. Maureen was from St. Ignace in the Upper Peninsula. We remained good friends through the years seeing each other at class reunions. We still keep in contact.

I went to Grand Rapids Junior College for a year and a half as part of the nurses training. After the first nine months of training, we started working as student nurses on the floor.

Received first nursing cap

During the time of training, we had a nurse's choir which I played for. I remember playing for a nurse's graduation probably during my junior year. Graduations were held at the historic Park Congregational Church downtown.

Jerry and I planned on getting married in February of 1958 because I would have a month off. He called in November of 1957 and said he had to go on a 5 month cruise in January. He would be home for Christmas and wanted to get married then. Mom said she didn't want a big wedding at Christmas but would give us the money for one.

We decided to marry and just have the immediate family. On December 29, 1957, we were married at the church. Rev. Albert Trembert married us. I wore a blue suit and hat and carried a white orchard on my white Bible.

Our wedding picture 1957

The minister kissed me at the end of the ceremony before Jerry could. I was quite shocked and surprised. After leaving the church, we went to Clifford Lake Inn for dinner. Then mom and dad drove us to Grand Rapids. We stayed at a hotel downtown. The next day we got on a train for Chicago and we stayed in Chicago until after New Year's Day. When we returned, we stayed at the cottage at Clifford Lake until he returned to the Navy and I went back to school.

I still had the month off in February, 1958. I went to Florida with mom and dad. It was cold that year and our motel wasn't even comfortable. We visited Cypress Gardens but I wore my winter coat there. The water skiers wore wet suits when they entertained. I visited the swimming pool in the shape of Florida that Esther Williams had used in her movie, "Dangerous When Wet." I loved her movies, her swimming, and her acting. When I was in high school I bought movie magazines at the drugstore where I worked and made a scrapbook of pictures and articles on her.

We visited Longboat Key, an island near St. Petersburg, Florida. We walked the beaches looking for shells. Longboat Keys is famous for its Sand Dollars which are my favorite shell. It is a shell that symbolizes Christ's life and death in 15 different ways. The following article was in the magazine, These Times, in April 1981. It was written by Ralph Blodgett as follows:

From generation to generation beachcombers around the world have handed down one of the most unique legends ever heard by human ears. It concerns a lowly seashell called the sand dollar, and the record it bears to the life, death, and resurrection of Jesus Christ.

However, contrary to most sea creatures, the sand dollar spends its entire life buried in the sand, utilizing a niche in nature that few other forms have invaded. It generally lives close to the shore, buried in the first few feet of the ocean floor and usually in a vertical position.

The top sand dollar is unusual. The bottom two is showing the two sides of the Sand Dollar.

The Legend of the Sand Dollar

There's a lovely little legend
That I would like to tell,
Of the birth and death of Jesus Christ
Found in this lowly shell.

If you will examine closely,
You'll see that you find here,
Four nail holes and a fifth one
Made by a Roman's spear.

On one side the Easter Lily,
Its center is the star,
That appeared unto the shepherds
And led them from afar.

The Christmas Poinsettia
Etched on the other side,
Reminds us of His birthday,
Our joyous Christmas tide.

Now break the center open
And here you will release,
The five white doves awaiting
To spread Good Will and Peace.

This simple little symbol,
Christ left for you and me,
To help to spread His Message
Through all eternity.

Before we left Florida, we drove down to the Florida Keys until we reached the city, Key West. Key West is the southernmost city in the continental United States. It was warmer there, I was able to swim in the ocean.

In our second year of nurses training, we started our specialty training. Each one was for three months. They included surgery, obstetrics, pediatrics and psychiatry. My training was all at Butterworth except for Psychiatric Training which was at Traverse City State Hospital. I learned to play euchre and pedro there. One of my patients was very agitated one day. She moved quickly to the bathroom, kicked a window and tried to cut her arm with a piece of glass. I yelled for help and she ended up with stitches only. We had keys on us at all times at the hospital because every door you went through was locked. We were allowed to work weekends at the local hospital, Munson Hospital. One weekend I had a young woman to take care of who had tried to commit suicide. She was critical. She was a previous patient at the State Hospital. We were paid for our time when we worked Munson. We were never paid at Butterworth, it was just part of the training.

At the end of my time at Traverse City, I was given an A grade in practice and a low grade for theory. My grades on tests were good, on one quiz, I believe I got a D. Butterworth didn't accept it, so I had to turn in my uniforms and move home. I had to drive to Grand Rapids for classes in psychiatry. Passed that with flying colors and I also did fine on the state boards. There were two other schools represented but Butterworth was toughest with requirements and 13 out of the 27 students had to take additional classes or some kind of reprimand. Traverse City State Hospital said we had been partying too much. I was married and I never went out with any gatherings. I stayed at the dorm and wrote letters to Jerry. So after I graduated, I had to make up time. I also had to make up the time they allowed me to take off for a few days when we were married.

I wrote Jerry a letter every day. He wrote me when he could. On the long 5 month cruise, he also went to Rio Janeiro, Brazil, Trinidad, Spain, Norway, England and into the Mediterranean Sea. He was discharged from the Navy late in the summer of 1958.

We found an apartment on Lyons Street near the hospital. Jerry got a job at Frank Edge Saw Co. downtown. They made band saws. Later, Phyllis lived with us in our apartment, while attending Davenport Business School during her second semester. She had been living in Esther Hall on Lyons Street for the first semester. At a later date, we finally decided to buy a house trailer and moved into a trailer park on the north end of town.

When my cousin Charlene married Roger Boorsma I played for the wedding. We were always close. Our mothers were pregnant for us at the same time. Char & Rog lived in the trailer park that we moved to. What good times we had with them. The men really enjoyed each other. For years to come, we visited each other often and went on little trips together.

They had a 19 foot cruiser boat that we went and stayed on. Roger always teased me for bringing too many suitcases and shoe boxes. Their yachts got bigger through the years. We would go visit them when Grand Haven had their Coast Guard Festival. We would be on the boat near the fireworks and watch the waltzing water show. One day as we were relaxing on the boat, Jerry said "Boors, I wonder what the poor people are doing today."

Jerry and I

Char and Rog

My sister, Phyllis married Warren a year later in January, 1959. They stopped to see us in Grand Rapids on their honeymoon. He was working for a plumbing company and she worked for an insurance company. They lived in Alma in an apartment. Eventually, they both went to college and finished their degrees. Warren in business and Phyllis became a commercial teacher.

One time I was working in the emergency room as a student

at Butterworth Hospital. We had a patient, the watchmaker, who had been slugged and pistol-whipped by a bandit in a jewelry store. $10,000's worth of jewelry was stolen. My picture was on the front page of the *The Grand Rapids Press* bandaging the watchmaker.

I graduated in September, 1959, and continued working at Butterworth after I made up my time I owed them. I was a charge nurse on a floor that had all private rooms.

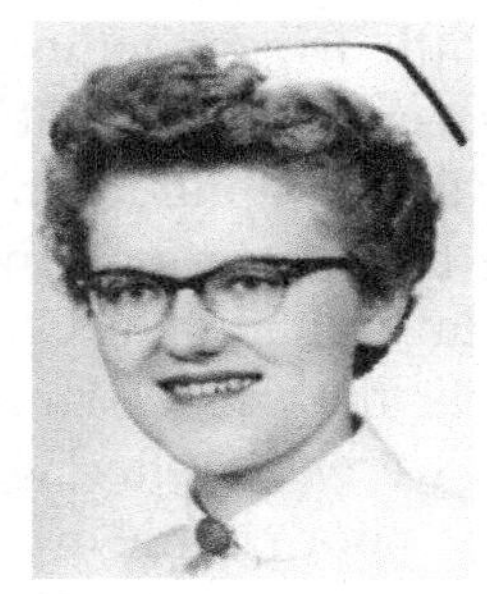

1959- Now a graduate nurse

Chapter 6

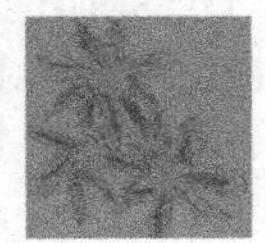

"Give thanks to the Lord, for he is good. His love endures forever." - Psalm 136:1

Back Home to Clifford Lake

The following year in April, we moved our trailer back to Stanton and lived at Clifford Lake on a lot my folks gave us. Jerry got a job at Belding Tool & Die and I got a nursing position with Dr. Gordon DeVries, a general practitioner in Stanton. Jerry worked in Belding about a year and then got a job at Greenville Tool & Die in Greenville. It was owned by Charlie Randall and Stanley Ash. He took courses for tool & die in Grand Rapids and finished at Montcalm Community College. He graduated from the first class that graduated at MCC. I worked as a nurse for Dr. Gordon DeVries for three years.

I remember watching Billy Graham crusades for many years on TV. I answered the call to Christ then. The first time as an adult. I requested the materials they sent out. I'm glad to have lived in the age of Billy Graham. A great man that God put on earth.

Our first child was a boy in July, 1963. We named him Scott Frederick Miller. His middle name was my father's name. I had done a study of a 5 month old child name Scott, in Pediatrics, who was diagnosed with Transposition of the Great Vessels. That was where the Aorta and the Pulmonary Arteries were reversed. I picked that name in memory of Scott that I had taken care of. He didn't live beyond five months of his life. I was due June 12 and delivered a month late. He weighed, 10 lb. 4 oz., 23 inches long. He could hold his head up when he was born. He had an early start. I stayed home with him for a while and Jerry continued to work at Greenville Tool & Die.

Scott at 5 months

Mother and dad lived across the street so they got to babysit quite often. They were still working at the plumbing and heating business in Stanton so they weren't available all the time.

When Scott was a few months old, I went to work nights at Sheridan Hospital. I worked there a few months until I got an opportunity to work as a county nurse. It was the days before our county had a health department.

The other nurse was a dear friend of the family, Mary Jane Lilly. She taught me everything she knew about community health. Our secretary was Beryl Gavitt. We traveled through the whole county following children with medical and orthopedic problems, patients with tuberculosis, visited doctor's offices, hospitals, and schools. We did pre-school clinics for all the schools every year going over health records and immunization records of all the children starting school.

One case I was involved with was an infant that had died. The physician called our office wanting one of our nurses to go see the infant at the funeral home. Mary Jane was away so I took some county supervisors with me. The funeral home was glad we came because it was a case of pure neglect. The details were very heart breaking. The infant's diaper area was completely raw. He had apparently been laying on his back for a prolonged time because the back of his head and the back of his heels were also raw. I had to testify in court when they were convicted and a second time after they were released from prison and wanted custody of their other children.

Around 1966, a state law required all counties to have health departments. We joined with Gratiot and Clinton County to become the Mid-Michigan District Health Department. Many children had never had immunizations so we had immunization clinics every month for years to catch kids up. Parents waited in long lines to have their children's immunizations. We helped in the other two counties at their clinics. Mary Jane moved out of state and I became the head nurse at Montcalm. My total time was 10 years working part-time and full-time. I hired Mildred Baldwin, who ended up staying there for many more years than I did. We took a lot of college courses from Western Michigan University at the same time. We became very good friends. We go to the same church so we still see each other often.

In 1966, we had another baby boy, Mark. His middle name was William, after Jerry's father, William (Bill) Miller. I went two weeks over. He weighed 10 lb. 12 oz. He was 22 ½ inches long. I told mother on the phone that he was ugly. She said, "He can't be." When she came to see him at the hospital. She said, "Oh my, he is." The reason was because he was full of fluid. He finally ended up being a handsome boy. He was quite shy at times and talkative at others. He cried for quite a few years when we sang, "Happy birthday" to him.

Mark at his first birthday

Angela at 3 years old

In 1969, we applied to adopt a little girl. Angela Marie was born March 31, 1970. She was a healthy 9 lb. 10 oz. Kay DeVries' cousin, named her daughter that, so I always remembered that name just in case we had a daughter. We got her when she was 6 days old. What a wonderful way to get a baby. You feel good and enjoy taking care of her. She always slept all night. She didn't have much hair until she was three.

I read a book by Corrie ten Boom, The Hiding Place. She was a Dutch Christian who, along with her father and other family members, helped many Jews escape the Nazi Holocaust during the Second World War she was imprisoned for her actions. "God does not have problems. Only plans," proclaimed Corrie when a clerical error allowed her to be released from a Nazi concentration camp one week before all women prisoners her age were executed. In 1971, her autobiography, The Hiding Place, became a movie in 1975, inspiring many to see God at work through the darkest of life's circumstances. Jerry and I and several members from church went to the Ionia Theater to watch it. I remember that during her days before she was taken to the concentration camp, she had memorized many Bible verses. These Words from God helped her through those terrifying times. This emphasizes the importance of memorizing verses. I always think of this when I think about Corrie ten Boom.

My friend, Mary Lou Miel married Gordon Johnson in our church that we had been raised in. I played the organ and Jerry sang. Mary had made her own wedding dress which was beautiful. They had two boys, Gordy and Chris. She was a speech pathologist in Southfield Public Schools for 15 years. My family and I enjoyed visiting her and her family often.

Mary Lou and Gordon came down to Sanibel Island in Florida every year and we enjoyed getting together. Mary and I dreamed about retiring down there and being able to see each other during the winter months.

Around 1975, I taught a high school health careers class for Greenville Public Schools at the hospital. I taught Anatomy and Physiology and a nurse aide course. On weekends, I started working part-time at the hospital. I was supervising over all the departments. It brought me back into hospital nursing which was good. I took a coronary care course. We never had anything like that when I was in nurses training in the 50's.

After that, I got a position at Central Montcalm Schools as a school nurse. My health department training was very useful. I liked working with the children. The hours were good because my children were going through their school years. I did that for three years and then I became the school nurse for Special Education in addition to Central Montcalm. So I kept busy going from school to school. In the spring, we had pre-school clinics. We met with parents and went over their immunization records and medical history. The hearing and vision technician also did tests on them. Back then, teachers and employees were required to have TB skin tests every year so I did them in the fall before school started. I became busy every fall checking students for head lice and helping families treat their children. We followed all the children with vision, hearing and health problems. I kept their health records up to date. There were always lots of first-aid to do and tending to sick children. The principal, Steve Strait, at Stanton Elementary, use to call me Doc Miller.

I was a certified CPR instructor, so I had classes for the teachers and several classes for students in all the schools for Central Montcalm and for the Montcalm Intermediate District.

Jerry worked at Greenville Tool & Die for sixteen years until we bought a welding business, G & N Equipment, in Grand Rapids with another business man who was good at sales. They built large welding tanks for dipping, like parts that needed to be chrome plated. We had that business for three years.

His partner was difficult to work with and he offered to purchase our half. We then purchased a sawmill from the Amish. We lived on the business from GR while getting the sawmill on its feet. It had six acres with a small sawmill and a small building used for a pallet shop and a maintenance building. Some of the Amish worked for us. I was the bookkeeper. We had the business for 22 years. Scott, Mark, and Angela all worked there most of those years. Jerry worked in sales, maintenance and built a couple of machines that were used in the pallet shop. When Jerry's health failed later on, Scott managed the sawmill. He also did a lot of the timber buying. Mark was a sawyer which means he brought logs in on chains, cut off the slab wood, the grade lumber and then the cant which makes up the stock lumber for pallets. This was all done by controls in a booth. Reminds you of airplane controls. At a later date, he became a grader. Mark also did much of the maintenance after Jerry wasn't able. Angela worked in the office but also made deliveries with the smaller trucks. She could load pallets or slab wood with the hi-low.

In 1982, we celebrated our 25th Anniversary with some of our family members.

Dad, Me, Jerry and Mom

My friend, Mary Lou developed breast cancer in 1983. She was treated regularly at MD Anderson Cancer Center in Houston, Texas. She had a lumpectomy and radiation. Later the cancer returned. She then had chemotherapy. She took a medical leave in 1985. After nearly three years, she developed bone cancer. She tried lots of alternative therapies to no avail. She even went to Germany and had injections that the actor, Yul Brynner, had tried. Nothing worked. On June 7, 1986, I was mowing the lawn on the tractor when Angela came out and told me Mary Lou had died. It was very traumatic loss to me. I will never get over it even though I know she is okay and is waiting for me to join her. It brings tears to my eyes every time I see her picture or think about her.

My dear friend, Mary Lou

In 1984, my dad wasn't feeling well while they were in Florida. He said there was something wrong with his head. I talked them into flying home so we could get some testing done. A CAT scan of the brain determined he had a brain tumor. I told Mom we will have to take it a day at a time. He had surgery. It was malignant. The neuro-surgeon told us he couldn't get it all, there were many feelers. After recovering from surgery, he had radiation and chemo. The radiation really took him down and he died four months later, in June 1984 at the age of 71 with the entire family at his side. He was a wonderful, quiet man and we all learned from his good and kind character.

The folks had planned on leaving their home on Clifford Lake and moving into Stanton to a home they owned. Jerry and I already had an option to buy their house on the lake. They planned on making the house in town into two apartments. So, the day of my father's funeral the family went in and looked at the house. My niece, Tina, said "Grandma, I don't want you to move to town". So we made plans to build her a new house across the road at the lake. We called her close friend, Frank Wykoff who was a builder. The new home was built shortly. She moved into her new home in November. She loved her new gardens and spent her winters in Florida.

Three years later, she married a Florida resident from Ohio, by the name of Jack Gerberry. They were both avid golfers. Mother had four Holes-in-One and he had three. They both sold their condos and purchased one on a golf course in Ft. Myers. Many years, Jerry and I would go stay with them at least two weeks and enjoyed playing golf often. We played other courses when we could. We enjoyed going to Ft. Myers Beach.

Chapter 7

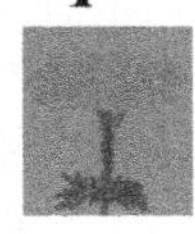

Abraham Lincoln- "One can complain because rose bushes have thorns, or rejoice because thorn bushes have roses."

Greenville Garden Club

My love for gardening came from my mother. She loved working in the garden. It would have been hard to find a weed in her flower garden.

Mother, Me, and grandson, Carlton

In the late 80's, mother and I were on the Holland Lake Golf Course League with Sue Remmy, Nancy Kortes and Bev Loding. Bev talked me into joining the Greenville Garden Club. Bev lived next to Sue at the time. I remember working a long day in Bev's garage making Christmas wreaths to sell for the club.

Many of us went to most of the District IV meetings and State conventions. We had great times together and learned many things such as flower arranging, care of bonsai trees, herbs, roses, perennials, making wreaths out of pine cones and other plant materials, and holiday arrangements. Anything that had do with gardening.

Sondra Fox, Sue Remmy, Nancy Kortes, and Me

The 1990 State Convention at Port Huron was great with Sondra Fox, Sue, Nancy, and me. Our husbands had a great time going golfing.

In 1990, I became vice president when Nancy was president and from 1992 -1994, I became president. I kept very busy with meetings, planning, and projects for the community. My daughter-in-law, Barbara, joined the club and we had fun doing window decorations in the Colony House for the Danish Festival for a few years. We had help from many of the other members. Greenville Garden Club is in District IV of the Federated Garden Clubs of

Michigan (Now the name is Michigan Garden Clubs, Inc.). There are seven districts in the state. We had a district meeting while I was president at Greenville.

Me and Nancy at our District IV Meeting

In 1993, the FGCM President, the District IV director and I presented Nancy with a Life Membership and in 1996, I received a Life Membership from the FGCM President.

Receiving Life Membership from FGCM President, Miriam Sanford

Nancy and I were asked to be on the state board. We went to the quarterly board meetings in Lansing. The first two years, we were project managers for the Meijer Gardens. We kept the Districts in the state notified of the project and raised monies for the garden. One of the projects was organizing each district to make a quilt to be raffled off at the state convention. I was not able to go at the time of the convention due to my illness and was not able to travel. I bought a few tickets and luckily, I won the District IV's quilt.

The beautiful quilt I won.

The next two years, Nancy and I were co-chairs of the 66th state convention which was held at Shanty Creek Resort in Bellaire, Michigan. A big project indeed. Getting speakers, programs, designs, table arrangements for the dinners, food and lodging. We had several meetings with other state officers and committee members. My sister helped out as secretary of the convention and helped me with planning and playing music. One of the days at the convention, she moved my scooter for me, lost control of it and tipped over a large potted tree that had been brought in for the convention. We laughed so hard.

The next two years, I was the Birds and Butterfly chairman and wrote articles for the state magazine every two months. It was educational for me to write these articles.

I still try to go to Greenville Garden Club monthly meetings when I can. Many of my close garden clubs friends have died. May they keep busy in heaven. We miss them so.

Chapter 8

"Rejoice in the Lord and be glad, you righteous; sing, all you who are upright!" - Psalm 32:11 NIV.

The Harmonettes Regroup

In 1984 Harmonettes started singing again and we performed in Kalamazoo and Lansing.
1985-Old Fashioned Days variety show was on stage near the hotel. Our MC was Steve Strait, the Stanton Elementary School principal, and the Central Montcalm Band Director, Mark Edwards, sang a number. Eric and Stacey Rolston played the piano. We were in the parade rode with Alvin Anderson in his convertible.

Phyllis, Arlene, Alvin Anderson, and Me

1986-Sang several numbers on stage during Old Fashioned Days.

Arlene, Phyllis, Larry Petersen, and Me

1986- "Christmas with the Harmonettes and Friends" was our first Christmas show. The proceeds benefiting the Central Montcalm marching band's trip to the college Gator Bowl game on December 27. Jerry and I went with the band as chaperones and I was the nurse along to help with any medical issues.

1987-I was a committee member and coordinated the variety show. We were scheduled to sing seven songs. My niece Tina Wells was a saxophone player from Central Montcalm High

School and performed a solo. The Old Fashioned Days show was dampened by rain. We performed on a small stage at Stanton Elementary School. There was a large crowd despite the weather. Our outfits were long Southern Belle dresses with matching umbrellas which were fitting with the rain.

1987 -The second Christmas show Larry Petersen was our master of ceremonies. He was with us many years at Old Fashioned Days Shows as the MC. We always enjoyed having him on with us.

We also, did a Christmas program which was open to the public at our church.

May 1988-Lowell Showboat in Lowell, MI- We performed as an opening act for the "The Lettermen," an American male pop music vocal trio that started in 1959.

Phyllis, Arlene, and Me

1988 Old Fashioned Days-Variety show featured '50s theme. "We were the hometown favorites," the Daily News newspaper said. Harmonettes were decked out in 50's attire and a juke box for atmosphere. We sang "Bye, Bye Love," "Goodnight Sweetheart," made popular by the McGuire Sisters back in the 50's, and "Mr. Sandman" made popular by The Chordettes and "Nevertheless." Nevertheless was a song from a Fred Astaire and

Vera-Ellen movie, "Three Little Words," a 1950 American musical film. "Nevertheless" (I'm in Love with You), was a 1931 song written by Kalmar and Ruby. It became our theme song and we finished each show with it. We had recorded it the previous fall, among other songs. It was recorded by Frank Sinatra and the Mill Brothers in 1950 and was performed by Dean Martin in 1955. At that time, Phyllis and I were both on the Old Fashioned Days Committee.

1988-September. We performed at the Amway Grand Hotel in Grand Rapids, Michigan. One time was for the Annual Meeting of the Supreme Council, 33 degree, Ancient Accepted Scottish Rite of Free Masonry for the Northern Masonic Jurisdiction of the US and another time was the Michigan Apple Convention.

1990-Harmonettes sang at Variety Show at Old Fashioned Days.

1991-Harmonettes sang at Variety Show-Old Fashioned Days.

1998-Harmonettes sang at Stanton Old Fashioned Days was an article in the Daily News. I was quoted, "When we're on stage, I love seeing the people enjoy our singing. If they're smiling, we're happy." One time I stated in an interview for the paper, "You know who likes to listen to us the most? Our mothers." At this point we had been singing for four decades. We enjoyed telling jokes and kidding around on stage.

2002-Harmonettes sang at Faith Lutheran Church, Sidney, Michigan.

Chapter 9

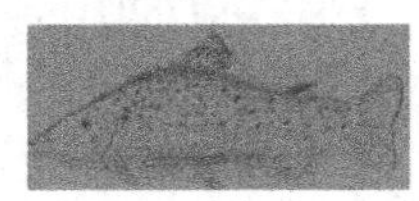

"And he said to them, "Follow me and I will make you fishers of men" - Matthew 4:19 ESV.

Thoughts about Jerry

In 1993, Jerry and I were golfing in Florida and he was having problems with his knees. When we got home, we followed up by seeing an orthopedic surgeon who said he had some arthritis and put him in a knee brace. He didn't tolerate this expensive device and continued to get worse. We finally went to Mayo Clinic in Rochester, Minnesota. He was diagnosed with rheumatoid arthritis. We got a rheumatologist in Grand Rapids. He went through many different kinds of treatment for rheumatoid arthritis. Nothing worked very well. We went back to Mayo a couple more times. Mayo put him on a new medicine that helped for a while. After four years with the rheumatologist in Grand Rapids, we found a new one in Okemos. At least this physician was a caring man and tried his best to keep Jerry comfortable.

Jerry still kept working for many years at the sawmill. He loved doing the maintenance work. Most of all, he loved to fish year round and hunt deer in the fall. One time he called me and was very excited about the deer he had shot. I said, "What are you going to do with that thing?" He was so upset with me with good reason. It was very unkind of me. I don't think I ever discouraged him about deer hunting after that but he always took his deer to his brother Bill's house to hang for skinning and cleaning. He did receive a Michigan Angler Award for a German brown trout and he had it mounted.

Scott and Jerry with their deer

Chapter 10

"For you have delivered me from death and my feet from stumbling, that I may walk before God in the light of life" - Psalm 56:13 NIV.

My Devastating Illness

It would be great to be prepared for everything life could throw at us. But no human has ever been prepared for everything, which was the case for me in February 1994. I did a breast exam while we were in Florida. I found a lump. I had been faithful about my yearly mammograms after Mary Lou had breast cancer. I was due to have one in March. I called the St. Mary's Breast Center in Grand Rapids. They had me come right in. After the mammogram and ultrasound, they said I needed to see a surgeon. I asked who was a good one down there. When we went back to the sawmill and told the kids, they were all very quiet, like they were in shock and didn't know what to say.

Dr. Stan Sherman did a breast biopsy and it was malignant. The lymph glands were negative. Mary Lou's had been negative.

I called MD Anderson in Texas where Mary Lou went for treatment. They would have taken me but they wanted me to stay down there for treatment. They said there are other cancer centers, like Mayo Clinic. I called Jerry's doctor there. He told me to come. It was winter so we flew to Rochester, Minnesota. I took my slides for a second opinion. They confirmed the malignancy. The treatment was similar so we returned to Grand Rapids. Dr. Sherman referred me to an oncologist, Dr. Mark Campbell who had trained at Mayo Clinic. The treatment was going to be chemotherapy and then radiation followed by more chemo. Dr. Campbell thought this was best in case there was something floating around. I started chemo in May. I was tolerating everything pretty well. I liked my chemo nurse, Barb Shaw, very much. I kept nurses notes for her each week which she really appreciated.

A Grand Rapids Press article written by a chemo nurse with breast cancer stated:

"I say, I trust the Lord no matter what. So he wanted me to put my money where my mouth is…I will trust him and he will take care of his own, and I know I am his child."

"I know the ultimate factor is God, you just have to rest in his care and in his word. He's not doing anything to harm you, and it's going to be OK. It might not come out the way you want

it, but if we trust in him, it's going to come out the way he wants it, and it's going to be OK – even in death." "I'm not afraid of dying," "I want to live long, and God knows that. I've got grandbabies and I want to see them grow and spoil them as a grandmother is supposed to do. But I know all of us have our time and only God knows."

The end of June, I wasn't feeling very well. My friend, Ardeth Steere said we had lunch at the Clifford Lake Inn just before the 4th of July and I wasn't myself. She said I was irritable. I thought it was the chemo making me feel so bad. I was having a low grade temp which the Cancer Center had me treat it with Tylenol. On July 4th, my sister had a dinner at their home next door. I couldn't eat very much so I went home and went to bed. The next day, I went for chemo. I told them I didn't want chemo unless they could tell me what was wrong. They drew extra blood and sent me home with no chemo. I think my white blood count was low that day too, so I might not have received chemo anyway.

Angela was to be married in two weeks and I needed to try my dress on so we went to Jacobsen's Department Store. When we got there, a courtesy wheelchair was available at the entrance. I said, "Jerry, I think I better get in that wheelchair because I feel so awful." I had to go down some steps and proceeded to try on my mother-to-be dress. After we left, we needed to stop and pick up my shoes that were being dyed. I asked Jerry to go in and get them. I didn't think I could make it. We drove home and I went right to bed. I took a nap. When I woke up and went to get up my feet were numb. I decided to walk across the road to mother's to wake up my feet. I don't think it helped. I laid down on her bed. When I got up, I went home and called the oncologist. He told me to go to ER at Butterworth Hospital in Grand Rapids. Jerry and my daughter-in-law, Barb, drove me. On the way, I told him to stop so I could lay down in the backseat. My back was hurting very much. I believe the muscles were getting weak already.

I was in ER for hours. My back was very painful. They gave me an injection of Morphine. I was hospitalized and they sent Jerry and Barb home around 3 a.m. Barb had to go to work in the early a.m.

I was admitted and put in a private room. About, 7 a.m., I called Jerry and told him to come back. I told him I didn't think I was going to make it. I remember very little after that. I do remember my friends, Joel Black and Tom Fritz coming. I don't even remember Jerry coming back. The neurologist came and at some point a spinal tab (lumbar puncture) was done. A small amount of fluid is withdrawn from the spinal canal in your lower back. I was soon diagnosed with Guillain-Barre' Syndrome. It is difficult to diagnose in its earliest stages. Its signs and symptoms are similar to those of other neurological disorders and may vary from person to person. Weakness and tingling in your extremities are usually the first symptoms. These sensations can quickly spread, eventually paralyzing your whole body. In its most severe form Guillain-Barre' Syndrome is a medical emergency.

In many cases, paralysis starts at the bottom of the lower extremities, the feet, and progresses upward. Mine went as far as it can go. Andy Griffith, the actor, had Guillain-Barre' and it went up to his waist. He had it at the age of 56, which was the age that I developed it. Joseph Heller, the author, writer, and playwright also had it and it started in the middle, moving upward and downward simultaneously.

Before many hours, I was placed into intensive care and placed on a ventilator, also known as a respirator, a machine that moves oxygen-enriched air in and out of your lungs. I was unable to breathe on my own. My body became immobile. I was completely paralyzed. Unable to move anything.

This ailment appeared early in modern medical writing as "Landry's ascending paralysis." In 1916 three Parisian physicians, Georges Guillain, Jean Alexander Barre', and Andre' Strohl added to this description of the characteristic anomaly they discovered of an elevation in protein in the spinal fluid of victims.

Guillain-Barre' Syndrome (pronounced Ghee-yan-Baa-ray-Sin-drome!) is a rare disorder that occurs in 1-2 patients per 100,000 population. We learned more about the illness from the GBS Foundation, (now named the GBS/CIDP Foundation), an organization, devoted to providing information, communicating with families similarly afflicted, and conducting research. The information was helpful to understand what was happening and this brought significant relief to my family. This is a life threatening disorder because it causes muscular weakness that can lead to difficulty breathing and swallowing. Any age group can be affected although it is more common in the 5th and 6th decades of life. About two thirds of patients are men and about one third are women. Most patients recover well although 20% develop persistent nerve damage with associated weakness such as difficulty walking. About 5 % die from it. Some remain severely disabled.

Guillain-Barre' Syndrome is the result of damage to the peripheral nerves that come off the spine. These include all of the cranial and spinal nerves. The cranial nerves control the movements of the mouth, cheeks, tongue and lips. The spinal nerves emerge from the vertebrae on both sides of the spinal column. All nerves send messages from your brain to the rest of your body. Nerves wear special jackets which help us pass messages down into every part of our body. In Guillain-Barre'

Snydrome, the jackets fall off and they can't send messages to tell your muscles to move. Sometimes it occurs after a tummy bug or a sore throat. It is caused by the patient's own immune system. This may be because the body system that fights illnesses is working so hard that it fights nerves by mistake. In approximately 60%-80% of patients the disorder is triggered by a preceding infection. In the USA 75% of these infections are respiratory, frequently due to Cytomegalovirus or Epstein Barr virus while 25% are triggered by diarrhea due most commonly to the bacterium, Campylobacter jejuni. In other areas of the world, poor sanitation results in many more cases of GBS from diarrheal infections. Other triggers include various vaccines, surgery, trauma, and autoimmune disorders.
1-The Communicator. GBS/CIDP Foundation International magazine, Spring 2013

This was the beginning of a three month stay in intensive care. I was on the respirator for the entire three months. After I was in intensive care, at some point, the Intensive Care physician in charge of my case, said to me that I would be more comfortable if they would put in a tracheotomy so they could take the big tube out of my mouth. A tube would be inserted directly into the trachea (windpipe). It reduces the risk of infection and decreases the risk of developing pneumonia. I shook my head to go ahead with it and I was taken to surgery for the procedure. I understood what a tracheotomy was because I had taken care of several patients with tracheotomies. I still have that scar from the tracheotomy in my neck.

I was unable to swallow liquids and foods. I went to surgery again on another day and a feeding tube that helped to sustain me was made by a unique puncture in my abdomen. They could give me some medications and a food formula through this tube. I remember working in the Diet Kitchen when I was in nurses training we made up the formulas using a blender. I remember that milk and bananas were some of the foods we used.

I developed pneumonia and I had x-rays daily for many weeks. I remained critical for a long time. Dr. Sherman, the breast surgeon, came to see me but he said later he didn't think I realized he was there. Dr. Campbell, the oncologist, came. He told me I wasn't doing very well. I don't remember what he said but I knew at that point I might not live through this. I prayed to God. I told him it wasn't up to me but was up to him if I was to live or not. I don't know if an angel came to me but a peace came over me and strengthened me. I knew if I didn't make it, I was going to be okay. Death is just a doorway. The whole burden was lifted off me.

Jesus prayed on the Mount of Olives. "Father, if you are willing, take this cup from me; yet not my will, but yours be done. An angel from heaven appeared to him and strengthened him" - Luke 22:42-43 NIV.

Jerry came every day, usually after work. He was still having problems with the rheumatoid arthritis. Sometimes he was so tired, he would pull off the road and sleep awhile. My illness probably didn't help his disease.

I don't remember much in the beginning after I was in ICU. A family member would stay all night with me. When family would come in and would speak to me, they really didn't know if I knew them. Nurses, respiratory therapists, physical therapists, radiology technicians were in the room all the time. The ICU nurse in charge of me was named Jan Reaves. A wonderful gal who I have kept in touch with all these years. My air mattress bed which cost $50,000 rotated my body, it was a constant movement to prevent bed sores.

I loved when it was time for a bed bath and backrubs were comforting.

Mom and Jack came almost every day. Jack kept a diary. Phyllis came every day that she could. My good friend, Nancy Kortes came often. She pretended she was family. Helga Kohl came and gave me a pedicure. Sue Remmy kept me in flowers. A nurse, Sue Rittenger, who worked with me when I was teaching health careers at United Memorial Hospital in Greenville, came to see me. Her sister had a similar experience. They called it a double stroke. A couple of previous Guillain-Barre' patients came to see me and talked with the family. Two of my classmates from our nursing class, Jan Elve, and Maxine DeGaynor came to see me. Most of the people that came I do not remember. I know the minister, Pastor Dave Engler and his wife, Barb, were faithful in coming often. When people came, I could only stand to listen to them a few minutes. It was hard to concentrate on what they were saying. It tired me so. Jerry's brother, Bill and his girlfriend, Katherine, came often. Dr. DeVries and Kay came often.

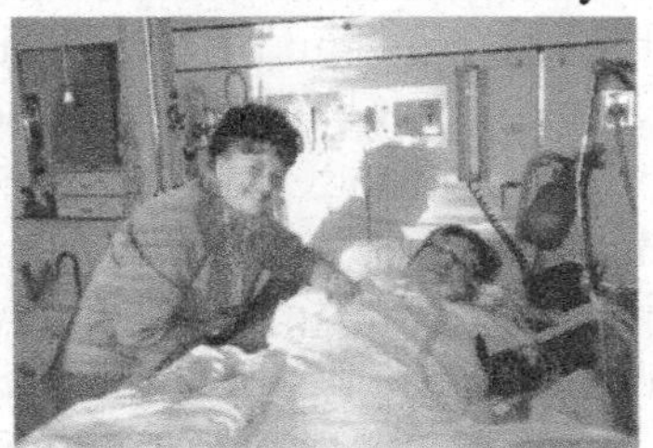

Kay and Me in intensive care.

I couldn't talk nor could I write. They used a board with a, e, i, o, & u. Each letter had a row of letters behind it. I communicated with my eyes as they pointed to each letter trying to make a word and then a sentence. One day mother and my step-dad, Jack were trying to do this. They would maybe figure out a word and move on to the next one. By the time we got that one done they would forget the previous one. So, we started over. I made them realize they needed to "w-r-i-t-e i-t d-o-w-n".

I had many other therapists. Occupational therapists and speech therapists. The respiratory therapists probably spent the most time tending to the respirator, working with my lungs because of pneumonias and drawing blood gases. They checked my blood gases to see how much oxygen was in the arteries. They did this on the inside of my wrists and it was very painful. I still have scars on my wrists. The work of preventing too many secretions was that they would lower the top of the bed and pound on my back to try and get secretions up. I wouldn't have lived without them.

The nurses took wonderful care of me and were in my room much of the time. I had tubes all over the place. I was turned every two hours or when I was uncomfortable. They were good about back care. Constipation is a problem when patients are bedridden for a sustained period. I had an embolism, a blood clot in the legs, a couple of times. This is an additional threat to anyone immobilized for long periods of time. The blood clot can break loose and go to the lungs. This can be fatal. They had long elastic pressure socks they put on me and they used the medication, Heparin, to help prevent blood clots. These injections were injected into the abdomen.

At some point, they transferred me to what I called a step chair. It was a way to start elevating my head and body to an upright position. They slid me over to the step chair which was placed alongside the bed with a bed sheet and 6 people. I hated the step chair. I had a call button that I squeezed in my neck area. I would call them and want to go back. They would usually say, "You can't go back to bed yet." They had to round up six people to transfer me back. What a chore for them. I was not a lightweight.

One time I was in the step chair. My elbow was on a

bedside stand. I was always belted in. My elbow fell off the stand and my upper body was hanging over the bed. I couldn't move and my bell had either slipped out or I wasn't able to work it. It's a wonder the respirator was still attached. Of course, I still couldn't call for help because of the respirator. What an experience! My friend, Char Boorsma, happened to come and visit me and found me hanging. She ran for help.

Another time the respirator quit. An alarm went off but it seemed a long time until they got there. The male nurse came running saying, "You would be in the last room." I was.

Very gradually I started regaining some movement. Facial expressions began to return. My step dad, Jack, would try to work with me and make me smile, frown, and wink. That was his job every time they came. I had to learn to touch my fingers to my thumb. Eventually I worked and got them all working.

I learned *patience.* Bob Dole, a previous Senator from Kansas stated, "Patience is learned in the hospital." He was badly wounded by German fire during World War II and had a lengthy recovery in the hospital. He received two Purple Hearts and a Bronze Star. You learn patience because you don't have a choice but to try and accept what you can and cannot do.

I lost 27 pounds totally even with the stomach tube.

After three months, they finally weaned me off the respirator. I was moved from intensive care to another area, a step down in care. I still had the tracheotomy in. One day, two physical therapists came to sit me up. The pain was so severe because the muscles were not working in my back. I screamed. Mother sat there crying. After they put me down, I told them to give me a pain pill an hour prior to doing that again. They took care of my request the next time, but it was still bad.

Another time they took me down to the Physical Therapy

Department. They strapped me on a table that stood me up. They were watching my blood pressure but I passed out. I don't remember going back to my room but after that I was having a lot of nightmares and hallucinations. One of the nightmares was we were in an upstairs apartment on the west side of the street in Greenville, watching the Danish Festival Parade and someone spilled a large kettle of split pea soup all over the floor and there was nowhere to walk. Another nightmare was I was on the ledge of a building and there was fire everywhere and I had no way to get down and be away from the fire. Then one of them, I was seeing many bugs crawl up the wall just right of the bed. Of course, there weren't any bugs. I said, "Jerry, you have got to get some bug spray." Jerry said to Angela, "What are we going to do?" Angela went in the bathroom and found a little spray bottle of some kind. She showed me the bottle and I said, "That's the good stuff, spray that." She pretended to spray the bugs with the bottle and made spraying noise. That seemed to calm me.

They moved my bed out by the nurse's station at night and mother would sit with me trying to calm me. The family got after the neurologist and they finally gave me something that brought me back to my senses. The only thing I could remember were the bad dreams. I still remember them.

The nurse, Jan, in charge of my care was a wonderful Seventh Day Adventist gal. They wanted to move me to Mary Free Bed Rehabilitation Hospital in Grand Rapids but they usually didn't take patients who still had the tracheotomy tube in. Jan's husband, John worked in administration at MFB, so I was soon transferred.

My stay at Mary Free Bed was nine weeks. My first roommate watched TV all night so I requested to be moved. I was put in a room by myself for quite a long time. Towards the end of my stay, I had a very dear lady that had been in a bad auto accident. We became good friends and I kept in touch with her. My physical therapist was Diane. She was really in charge of that the Physical Therapy department there at Mary Free Bed. I never saw her working with anyone else but me. I always thought my special treatment was set up by John Reaves (Jan's husband) in administration. I had good nursing care there as well. I had P.T. and occupational therapy 5 days a week.

Weekends were boring although I had some therapy on Saturdays in my room. TV was very limited on the weekend with sports shows or hunting and fishing shows. I never remember reading because it was very tiring just to hold a book. I learned how to brush my own teeth and how to dress myself. Getting in and out of a bed, it took a gait belt, a slide board and of couple of assistants to help. I eventually was able to use a wheelchair. After going down to therapy, they would say, wheel yourself back upstairs. I would go down the long hall, up the elevator and down more long halls to my room with little pushes at a time. It took me a long time and was very exhausting. When I got back, I would ask to go to bed. They would say you need to sit in the wheelchair at least fifteen more minutes. I didn't like that. It was so tiring. I was introduced to pool therapy there. I wasn't able to do much but the water felt good.

I had a couple of outings. They took me shopping at Rogers Dept. Store and I bought a new winter coat. One time a group of us went to the Schnitzelbank, a German restaurant, across the parking lot. Jerry went too. We probably told them the story of our first wedding anniversary dinner. We were living in a trailer park on the north side of Grand Rapids. I was still in nurses training. We went to the Schnitzelbank Restaurant for dinner. When we got there, I discovered I had changed purses and the money was at home. We told them we wouldn't be able to order. We went home and got the money but we were so embarrassed we didn't go back there. We went to a different restaurant called Holly's.

Jerry came to see me every day at Mary Free Bed for those nine weeks except 2 or 3 days when he went deer hunting. He came down after he got done working. Sometimes he slept after he got there to see me. He would often lean over the railing of the bed but his body movements were too much for me. It would stir up my nerve endings, so I would have to tell him you can't do that. I would feel bad to have to say anything. I know it was probably hard for him to understand because he didn't feel like he was moving. It didn't take much to throw me into a very uncomfortable feeling.

I was having occupational therapy, also. I tried to do some typing but was not successful at that. I did address all of our Christmas cards. It was slow and my penmanship wasn't the greatest, but I did finally finish them. I had to go to their kitchen and try to make different foods. I wasn't up to that either but whatever they wanted, I tried to accomplish it.

Angela, Phyllis, Me, and my niece, Tina

After nine weeks, I had a day visit at home. The family had balloons and flowers waiting for me. It seemed so good. Mary Free Bed required that I had to have two exit ramps out of the house. Jerry had to make an extra exit accessible for me to get out in case of an emergency. The occupational therapist came with me to check out our house.

I was surrounded with loving support from so many with encouragement and prayer. I am convinced they helped in my healing process. For instance, some of the gals from the Greenville Garden Club came and planted pansies along my drive when it got warm enough.

Chapter 11

"Be strong and courageous. Do not be afraid; do not be discouraged, for the Lord your God will be with you wherever you go" Deut 31:6 NIV.

Rehabilitation for Two Years Plus

I finally was discharged a couple of days before Christmas. I don't remember much about that holiday time. I'm sure it was exhausting but wonderful at the same time. I started physical therapy at Kim O'Donald's in Greenville a few days after Christmas. Originally, Mary Free Bed wanted me to come down there for out-patient therapy but it would have been a long ride for me and hard on Jerry. Going to Kim O'Donald's was about a twenty minute drive. I knew Kim from my school nursing days when we were both working for Special Education. This was before she started her own business. Kim had worked with cases with the nervous system. She was in charge of my case.

Me, Leslie, and Annette

Physical therapists, P.T. assistants and an Occupational therapist also worked with me three days a week at her office and two days a week at the college pool. The sessions ran from one to two hours a day.

To get in the car, I had to be transferred on a sliding board. It took two people to push and pull to get me on the transfer board and out of the wheelchair and into the car. Then reverse the push and pull out of the car into the wheelchair. One person was in the driver's seat and one pushing or pulling by the wheelchair. A transfer board is a manufactured piece of lacquered wood, beveled at both ends and about twelve inches wide and twenty-four inches long.

The sessions at therapy were tiring and sometimes painful. It was a matter of training all muscles from the neck down. I had to learn to sit up independently. They rented a machine that helped my body to be in a standing position similar to the one they used at Butterworth Hospital. My body was strapped in as well as my feet. They would take my blood pressure to see if I could tolerate it and they kept increasing the time.

I did enjoy the pool with a lift that put me down in the water.

Two people would work with me, trying to teach me to walk in the water and many passive exercises. Eventually I was able to try and swim. I had always been a good swimmer and did love swimming all my life. I was fortunate to have been brought up on a lake. Swimming was never hard to do even then.

When difficulty comes our way and we're called to walk through some dark and fearful valleys, our greatest help can come from those whom God has given to us, as a spouse. In the husband-wife relationship there is an intimacy that can be the source of great encouragement. God calls us "suitable helpers" for one another, and that means providing steadiness and encouragement for each other when our times of trial and testing come. When husbands and wives love each other, the one who suffers has a faithful supporter.

It is amazing what people will do out of love for another. As you take your wedding vows to care for each other in sickness and health, you don't realize what it might involve.

Jerry bathed, clothed, and transported me from the bed with a lift to the wheelchair, from the wheelchair to a recliner, and from the wheelchair in a sling to the bathtub. He was unable to lower it enough to actually get me in the tub but I was showered right in the sling. He sacrificed energy and sleep, suffered pain himself to get up at night to put me on the bedpan sometimes several times a night.

A special cousin of mine, Joan Thurber Sturm, flew here from Ohio, to spend a few days with me. She took me to physical therapy and got some meals ready for us. That was a big help to Jerry. She has always been a very dear relative. We have kept in touch all these years since we were young. Lots of happy memories. When we were young, many holidays were spent at their house or ours. Family is a closeness that neither time nor distance can diminish.

After about a year, the neurologist ordered that I be fitted with braces. They are made of a hard plastic with straps called AFO's (ankle foot orthotics). They are molded to fit the bottom of the foot and go up the back of the legs to just below the knees. There was no joint at the ankle. I wouldn't have had strength in the ankles to stand. I started by taking steps on the parallel bars. I had to wear gloves because the hands were too sensitive for the chrome bars. They always had a belt on me with one or two people to help me to learn to take steps. Later, I was fit into AFO braces with hinges which helped with balancing on uneven surfaces.

The physical therapists worked with passive exercises and stretches. Different machines were used during the two plus years. The occupational therapist worked with my arms, fingers, and hands. I also practiced activities for working in the home such as lifting towels or dishes up into a cupboard. I had so much sensitivity in my fingers that when I went to a restaurant and they brought ice water, I would have to ask them to bring me a glass of water with no ice.

I know I didn't like everything I had to do. I knew I didn't have much of a choice. I had to work towards getting well. If I hadn't gone through the therapy, I would have had to be dependent on family for everything or ended up in a nursing home. Jerry wasn't well enough to take care of me full time.

I learned patience by being patient. Patience before the Lord just may be the greatest single benefit of any such experience. When we learn that, we're growing while we're healing. When I was discharged from the hospital and going to therapy, we would need to get groceries. I would wait in the car for Jerry because it was too much work to get me out of the vehicle. So I would sit there and be patient. I would have never been able to sit and be patient prior to the illness. *"Be still before the Lord and wait patiently for Him" - Psalm 37:7a NIV.*

Chapter 12

"For the Spirit God gave us does not make us timid, but gives us power, love and self-discipline"
2 Timothy 1:7 NIV.

11,000 Miles

After two years, the neurologist decided I had had enough therapy for the time being. They had all been good to me and very patient with me. We decided to go on a trip to the southwest because we had never been there. We had some friends that lived in Arizona. We found a one-bedroom condo to stay for a month. It had a heated pool which we took advantage of. We met a couple there and did a few things with them. I wasn't driving much yet except on the expressway. I had hand controls on the van by them.

After Arizona we went to San Diego, California to see my high school friend, Christa Hansen. She was a teacher who had recently retired. We spent a few days near her. We went to San Diego Zoo and went to a musical. She was a great hostess. We drove up to see some longtime friends, Ken and Dotty Whiting who lived at Oceanside, California. They had a nice dinner for us. After dinner, we drove to the ocean to watch the sunset.

After we left California, we headed to Texas. Jerry's brother, Bill and Katherine were staying there near Brownsville. We visited Pedra Island and went into Mexico for a short shopping trip. We also went to see my niece, Tina and her boyfriend, Scott Dozier. We had a great time with them. They took us to the Alamo and the famous, Riverwalk.

Mark, Me and Jerry

Because the sawmill needed a grader that could grade our grade lumber before it was sold Scott wanted Mark to go to The National Hardwoods School. So, he went to school in Memphis, Tennessee for about three months to learn to be a grader. A grader stands at the end of many chains and decides what kind of wood it is and the footage in each piece. He also learned about drying lumber in a kiln.

After Texas, we headed to Florida by the way of Memphis, Tennessee to see Mark. We spent a day with him and then headed to Florida.

We spent a month at the Hideaway Condos in Ft. Myers, where mother and Jack lived in the winters. We rented a condo there and became good friends of a couple who lived above us. Bill and Katherine came and stayed with us after they left Texas. The men loved to go fishing. We had a fish fry for my folks and our new neighbors upstairs. We traveled totally 1,100 miles.

Getting together with close friends was part of our good life.

Larry and Sheila Camp, Jerry and me, Tom and Joyce Fritz.

Chapter 13

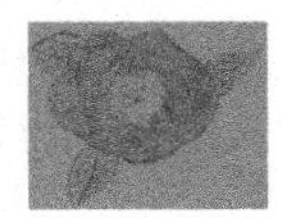

"I can do all this through him who gives me strength" - Philippians 4:13 NIV.

More Life Struggles

Eventually, I went back to work at the sawmill. I got so I would drive up close to the steps and get myself in to the office with a walker. My desk chair had wheels on it so I shoved myself around the office much of the time.

Scott, thought maybe we should buy a handicap accessible vacation trailer. One I could get in and out of. We searched until we found one that I could use the toilet, shower, and a queen size bed for sleeping. I had a recliner for watching TV. Jerry slept on the fold out in the living room. We added a foam mattress topper to give him more comfort. We also had to buy a vehicle that would haul the trailer which was 36 ft. long. My scooter that fit in the van was too large for the Suburban. So we purchased a smaller one that would fit. Scott and Barb paid half and used it in the summer on small trips and we took it to Florida. We drove it to Fort Myers, Florida and stayed in Siesta Bay RV Park on the mainland near Sanibel Island. We enjoyed some of the activities of the park like swimming in the pool, playing euchre and going over to the Hideaway condos to visit my folks and our friends that lived there in the winter. We went there a couple of winters, then we decided to find a double wide home in a park. We found a nice gated community in North Fort Myers. We had Billy and Katherine bring down the van and take the trailer home. They stayed with us a few days. I really enjoyed furnishing some new things for our home and having some family and friends come south to visit us. I'm not sure how much Jerry liked the shopping but he loved the company that came. We did some landscaping outside with plants that would grow in the south.

Our place in North Ft. Myers, FL

The next few years, we kept busy at the sawmill. I would go in and work at the office every day and Jerry would work in the maintenance shop. Often though near the end of the day we would go to Grand Rapids and pick up parts. Maintenance is continuous with so many machines.

Life seemed good except for Jerry with his rheumatoid arthritis. My strength got stronger in time, though nerves heal at a very slow pace.

Jerry developed other problems such as losing the central vision in one eye from a stroke in the eye called a central retinal venous occlusion. He still had peripheral vision which helped him to drive. There was no treatment then and it happened within a couple of days. He developed heart problems. His cholesterol and triglyceride were hard to control. He developed diabetes from the long use of steroids for the rheumatoid arthritis. He developed spinal problems but the neurologist said he wouldn't do surgery on him with his multiple problems. As the years went by, Jerry was able to do less. He would fish and hunt if he was up to it. He loved going to church. He loved our pastor, Jamey Nichols. Pastor Jamey always enjoyed him. When Jerry went fishing or hunting with him, they never had much luck. They probably were talking too much.

In February 2004 we were forced to close the business. It was a traumatic loss to us after being in business for 22 years. We had to let our 30 plus employees go. It was hard on the whole family. There was an auction and everything was sold for so little and some of the equipment was stolen. There was no way to prove it. The land and buildings were sold. We eventually lost our home on the lake.

We moved into mother's home. She was in an assisted living home. She remained there until she died at the age of 90.

Chapter 14

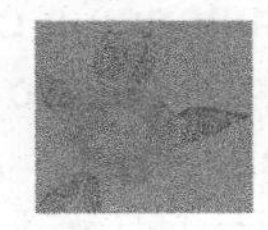

"Come to me, all you who are weary and burdened, and I will give you rest" - Matthew 11:28 NIV.

My Husband's Life Ends

Jerry's health declined. He spent most of his time in bed. He got up for meals and sometimes he would go out to the garage. He would sit on a stool and do whatever he could. When he had appointments with the doctors, sometimes he couldn't get himself in or out of the house. Of course, I was of little help. A good friend, Joel Black came and helped me many times to get him in the van or back in the house after we got home.

Finally tests showed that he needed some surgical heart procedures done including replacing the aortic valve, ablation procedure and coronary bypasses.

He was scheduled early in May 2006 for surgery. We try to have faith when facing possible death. We try to brace ourselves and prepare, but still we tremble in our weaker moments. Jesus gives us peace that we cannot find from within, but that carries us at our weakest times.

He survived the surgery and was critical for at least a couple of weeks at Meijer Heart Center in Grand Rapids. Later he was transferred to Kent Community Hospital. He needed skilled nursing care and rehabilitation. He was never comfortable. He did walk in the hallway with assistance a couple of times. He always felt like he couldn't get his breath. He told Phyllis and Warren, he wished he had never had the surgery. Later he was transferred to the Masonic Pathways Rehabilitation Center in Alma, MI for about five days. He turned critical again with congestive heart failure and pneumonia. He was taken to Alma Hospital and placed in intensive care for a few days until I insisted that he be returned to the Heart Center in Grand Rapids. At Meijer Heart Center they found his new heart valve was infected. He still had pneumonia and congestive heart failure. He was there for about a week then they moved him back to Masonic Pathways.

About 4 days later, I was on my way to see him when I got a call that he was is ER at Alma Hospital and the doctor wanted to talk to me. Jerry actually was gone, the catscan of the brain showed no activity. He was placed on a respirator, we left him on it until the family could all arrive. He died on July 31, 2006. My sister, Phyllis, Jerry's brother, Bill, and Pastor Jamey were with me there all day. Going through another trial of life again was very difficult, but God takes over. He supplies you with his love and strength. I was tired from driving for those months everyday but I was okay, too. I don't remember everyone who came to visitations and the funeral. You try your best to be cordial. Everyone is so kind and caring. It is hard to absorb those days and days that follow. My life of Jerry caring for me and my life caring for him had ended. Now it was up to me.

"Rejoice with those who rejoice; mourn with those who mourn"
Romans 12:15 NIV.

The Holy Spirit comforts us in our times of sorrow, and we are able to bring that comfort to others. That doesn't mean we show up to cheer them up. On the contrary, we come alongside those who weep to show the love of Jesus to them and weep with them. It will be Jesus, who takes the tears away.

Life is often touched by sorrow, and no good can come of getting bogged down in feeling hopelessly sorry for ourselves.

In the midst of losing a loved one, we can be thankful for the gifts of life they shared with us while they were in this world.

I know that death is not the end for us. I have confidence that Christ has overcome death, and He promises a glorious resurrection and eternal life with Him. We know that the loved ones we lose in Christ are not lost to us forever. Praise to You, Jesus, for overcoming death and the grave for us!

Even in my pain, I hold close to my heart the gift of my life with Jerry. The memory of him is a part of my life forever.

I have close friends who have lost their husbands. I have stayed close to them to try and help them in their grief. I will care for others who may need my help in any way that I can help.

"The most trying situations we face have to do with sickness, injury, financial problems, marital strife, relational difficulties, work-related challenges, and, the worst, the passing of someone you love or facing your own impending death. We need to know that God is with us during these terribly upsetting times. We have to be sure that we can stand

strong, no matter what is happening."
1-Stormie Omartian, The Power of a Praying Life, Harvest House Publishers, 2010, pg. 221.

"The problem is that we often forget to hold on to God's hand and depend on Him for every step we take. We think that if God will just get us over this hump, we can handle it from here."
2-Omartian, pg. 221.

If all the planning of my life was totally in my hands, I would not have chosen disappointments, changed plans, interruptions, sorrows and sicknesses, but I must admit that my life has had many blessings, surprises, and growth experiences. It is important for all of us to understand the number of days we receive on this earth is not determined by fate or whim, but by God. Similarly, it is important to understand that the content of those days is also in the hands of the Lord. How reassuring! But the challenge is for us to trust Him totally, and make the most of every day and every experience He provides for us.

As we age in later years, we may experience a decline in personality, intellect, or ability. Illness and frailty may set in. My friend, Joanne said, "I've never been this old before." The passage of time brings changes, not all of them good. We can begin a day, a year, or a career with vigor, enthusiasm, health, and hope, only to experience exhaustion, pessimism, sickness, and despair later. We don't plan for those disappointments to happen, but they do.

In the fall of 2006, my sister, Phyllis, asked if I would join her in starting a music studio in Stanton. I agreed because I had more time then I had previously when Jerry was alive. We started teaching piano, organ, and voice lessons. I could teach accordion, also. She hired a guitar teacher because we never played a guitar. Prior to this, she had been teaching in her home and I had taught in my home but it had been many years back for me. We both had always wanted to play a violin but never discussed it with each other. We probably wanted to because Grandpa Hansen played so well. We purchased violins and taught ourselves. Phyllis took a few lessons. We played and practiced together for many hours and days then we started teaching students.

At church, I stayed active in playing the piano, singing in the choir, and Phyllis and I filled in when the organist was gone. I was in the Women's Fellowship, on the Diaconate and lead several Bible studies. I did four sermons when Pastor Jamey was gone. I wanted to do what I could do for God and the church. He had done so much for me, to keep me going.

I joined the Eastern Stars and became the organist. I play the piano for different parts of our meetings. The Order of the Eastern Star is a Freemasonic appendant body open to men and women. The order is based on teachings from the Bible, and is open to all religious beliefs.

I developed macular degeneration several years ago and glaucoma last year. I have gone to a local low vision support group that meets monthly. I started going thinking I might learn something that would help me in the future. There is an excellent book, Practical Strategies for Living with Vision Loss, by Peggy R. Wolfe. I now have the 2nd edition. I highly recommend this book and the support group for anyone experiencing some vision problems. Developing positive attitudes of acceptance, patience, enthusiasm and gratitude is very important in any physical disability or illness.

Chapter 15

"Be kind and compassionate to one another, forgiving each other, just as in Christ God forgave you"
Ephesians 4:32 NIV.

My Wonderful Siblings

In 2015, my sister, Phyllis and her husband, Warren Wells were the Grand Marshals for Stanton's Old Fashioned Days. Warren and a group of other businessmen had formed a committee back in the 1980's to start up Old Fashioned Days. It was based on memories of the Anniversary Days in the 50's. So in the 80's, Stanton Old Fashioned Days became the festival every year in the summer. Phyllis and Warren served on the committee for years. I was on it for four years and was in charge of the talent show.

Warren and Phyllis Wells

Phyllis did it more years and it was named Star Quest. Jerry and I worked on the parade one or two years. Phyllis did the parade, too, for many years. Phyllis and Warren have spent a lifetime giving back to the community they love. They were very deserving of this honor.

My brother, Lloyd Hansen, and his wife, Judy recently moved from Williamsburg, Virginia to Grand Rapids, Michigan. They had more family in Michigan and they have a great love for Michigan State basketball and football. Lloyd spends much of his leisure time golfing and Judy is a magnificent quilter. She has a website: http://smallquiltsanddollquilts.blogspot.com.
It is great having them living closer.

Lloyd and Judy

Chapter 16

"Heaven and earth will pass away, but my words will never pass away"- Matthew 24:35 NIV.

Reading the Bible

Reading the Bible is much easier to understand than I ever thought. Especially with the newer versions. I really prefer the New International Version. Sometimes, I look at other versions to see if I can understand it better. I like using Bible Gateway on my iPad. It is easy to find a verse quickly and check other versions. Recently our minister said, "The Author of the Bible is God." It is such a blessing, in this day and age, to have the privilege for us to be able to freely be able to read this book written so many years ago.

Another great source I have enjoyed and have encouraged people to read is a daily devotional, "Teach Me To Pray," by Andrew Murray. Andrew Murray lived most of his life in the nineteeth century but he has much to say to Christians of the twenty-first century. His extensive writings encourage a fully committed deeply personal relationship with Jesus Christ. He was born in Cape Town, South Africa, in 1828. He was a South African writer, teacher, and Christian pastor. His missionary and evangelistic work was highly recognized and he authored 240 books.

Attending Bible studies is a great source of learning. I have taught a few Bible studies, most of them were by Beth Moore. They included a Bible study book and DVD presentation with each series. My favorite is "Living Beyond Yourself – Exploring the Fruit of the Spirit" by Beth Moore.

"But the fruit of the Spirit is love, joy, peace, forbearance, kindness, goodness, faithfulness, gentleness and self-control. Against such things there is no law"- Galatians 5:22-23 NIV.

Read John 15, Jesus describes us as being rooted in Him. He is the vine, the support system and stability of our faith. What it shows to everyone else are the fruits of faith, but underneath that growth is the massive root system, fed by the Lord himself.

At times, however, we cut ourselves off from our root system when we skip worship or neglect God's Word. Then our faith shrivels. But God still invites us to be nourished by His gifts. As we meditate on God's Word, we learn more deeply about God's promises to us.

"Salvation is not from the Scriptures themselves but from faith in Christ Jesus. Scripture is to teach us where to find the source of all light and knowledge and can only direct us to something better."
1–Andrew Murray, Teach Me to Pray, Daily Devotional Insights, Barbour Publishing, August 11 Reading.

"For everything that was written in the past was written to teach us, so that through the endurance taught in the Scriptures and the encouragement they provide we might have hope" - Romans 15:4 NIV.

And only by reading God's Word can we see what we do wrong.

A few reasons to read the Bible and let his Word live in you:

1. To have your prayers heard.
2. To have your prayers answered.
3. To be on a path that leads away from death. *"In the path of righteous is life, and in its pathway there is no death" Proverbs 12:28 ESV.*
4. To have peace, *"Great peace have those who love your law, and nothing can make them stumble" - Psalm 119:165 NIV.*

"It is extremely important to understand that reading God's Word doesn't make us righteous. We are considered righteous by God because of what Jesus has done, not anything we have done."
3 – Omartian, pg. 48.

Abraham Lincoln said, "After a great deal of study of the scriptures, your Christian faith is inspired."

Chapter 17

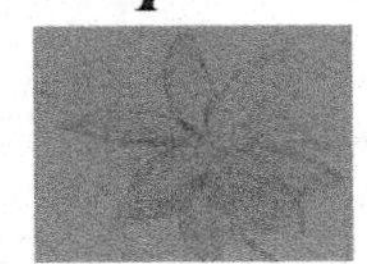

"But may the righteous be glad and rejoice before God; may they be happy and joyful." Psalm 68:3 NIV

Joy and Happiness

I remember seeing this song in Sunday school:

I've got the joy, joy, joy
Down in my heart (Where?)
Down in my heart (Where?)
Down in my heart
I've got the joy, joy, joy, joy
Down in my heart
Down in my heart to stay.
And I'm so happy
So very happy

I have the love of Jesus in my heart
(down in my heart)
And I'm so happy
So very happy
I have the love of Jesus in my heart.

Happiness is hard to define. To me, it is loving others and being loved by Jesus who gave his life for me. I am happy that the Holy Spirit lives in me and helps me in my daily life and relationships with others.

My son recently said to me one day, "Be nice, Momma." That is true, I must be nice to others in a loving way, for them to love me. If I am not happy, it can affect others.

"A cheerful heart does good like medicine, but a broken spirit makes one sick"Proverbs 17: 22 TLB.

Our happiness and joy are not dependent on whether or not other people do what we want them to do. We may never be able to influence anyone else to do what we think is right. But with God's help, we can change ourselves to bring about the results we want in life. Accept others for who they are and see how God works in you to complete your joy.

"God wants us to laugh. Jesus wants us to experience His joy, not just preach about it, or read books about it. Don't hesitate to laugh when you suddenly feel joyful; you will quickly find that joy is very contagious."

1-Joyce Meyer, Starting Your Day Right, Devotions for Each Morning of the Year, Faith Works,1987 pg198

The joy of my life is my God, my husband, my children, and my grandchildren. How I look forward for them to call, text, or come to visit. During the holidays, I plan well for their presence. At first, I didn't want any part of Facebook, but my granddaughter, Katlin, kept after me and I finally gave in. She set everything up and now it is also part of my life and my joy. To see pictures of my friends and relatives is a great part of this new technical world. I love to see their comments and their kindness and politeness saying, "*Thank-you and love you.*"

We are encouraged in our faith by the presence of Christian friends and other believers, like when we go to church, and we become a blessing to them also.

The church is a joy of my life. The kindness, help and love shown to me, the sermons, and the music have uplifted me. My friends at church are truly good people. How wonderful we have a place to worship our Savior.

"A cheerful heart is good medicine, but a crushed spirit dries up the bones" Proverbs 17:22 NIV.

"Take delight in the Lord, and he will give you the desire of your heart" Psalm 37:4 NIV.

Chapter 18

"Therefore, my brothers and sister, make every effort to confirrm your calling and election. For if you do these things, you will neer stumble" - 2 Peter 1:10 NIV.

Doing God's Work

I love knowing the Lord. I love people. I want to care for people as they have cared for me. I'm not perfect but I want to do my best to ensure that I am living a life that is pleasing to God.

I have a true desire to help people and do for others. By doing the work Christ wants us to do, it makes us feel good, blessed and possibly better than those we help. It is not only what he wants me to do, it's what I want.

I enjoy serving him in music, playing the piano and organ or singing in the choir. I enjoy listening to the sermon, and praying for others in need. Once someone said, "You don't have to be at church every time the door opens," but I try to be there as much as I can. The Holy Spirit encourages us to be there.

I had the experience of doing four sermons at the church in the past and I did enjoy studying and preparing for them. I pray they were encouraging to the church members. It was a good learning experience for me.

One of the several ways in which God helps our weak faith is by raising up and sending out pastors to teach us the His Word. As shepherds lead their sheep to feed in green pastures, so our pastors lead us, God's sheep, to feed our faith in the Word of God.

"Let us not become weary in doing good, for at the proper time we will reap a harvest if we do not give up. Therefore, as we have opportunity, let us do good to all people, especially to those who belong to the family of believers"- Galatians 6:9-10 NIV.

We need to have our mind full of ways to bless people. Early in the day, think up something you can do to surprise somebody or to make someone happy. You will be amazed at how quickly the Lord leads you to something good you can do for someone.

"For we are God's handiwork, created in Christ Jesus to do good works, which God prepared in advance for us to do" - Ephesians 2:10 NIV.

Chapter 19

"Truly my soul finds rest in God; my salvation comes from him" - Psalm 62:1 NIV.

Salvation

I feel so blessed that I accepted Christ as my Savior so many years ago and the way it has taken me through the good and the bad.

To understand God, it starts with the desire to know Him and then as time goes on, you will want to know Him better. Eventually as you grow, you will want more and more of Him in your heart and in your life.

Are you certain that your sins are forgiven and that heaven will be your home? This question is extremely important. If you are not certain of salvation, you must either run away from the realities of life or run away from the inevitable fear of death. Following this path, you will live in tormenting doubt and agonizing insecurity.

"We all have something we are guilty of at some time. Whether we feel guilty about the things we know we have done wrong or regret over what we feel we should have done better. Our shoulders were not built to carry guilt. It weighs us down and breaks us.

We may have a longing to 'do over' some things in our life. We can refuse to think about it, but it will surface at some point, in some manner anyway. And it can make us sick, miserable, angry, or depressed. However, when we receive Jesus, we are cleansed completely from our past. That means every mistake or violation of God's rules, ways, or laws is completely forgiven. The slate is wiped clean."
4-Omartian, pg. 28

If you want to receive Jesus, take these four simple steps:

1. *Believe that Jesus is who He said He is, Jesus* said, "I am the way, the truth, and the life. No one comes to the Father except through Me" - John 14:6 NIV. Say, *"Jesus I believe You are the Son of God, as You say You are."*
2. *Declare that Jesus died on the cross and was resurrected from the dead.* "If you confess with your mouth the Lord Jesus and believe in your heart that God has raised Him from the dead, you will be saved" - Romans 10:9 NIV. Say, *"Jesus, I believe You laid down Your life on the cross and were resurrected from the dead to live forever so that I can have eternal life with You."*

3. *Confess and repent your sins and failings.* "If we claim to be without sin, we deceive ourselves and the truth is not in us. If we confess our sins, he is faithful and just and will forgive us our sins and purify as from all unrighteousness" 1 John 1:8-9 NIV.

Say, "Lord, I confess my sins and failings and I repent of them. I ask You to help me live Your way now so that I can become all You created me to be."

***4. Ask Jesus to live in you and fill you with His Holy Spirit, and thank Him that you are now God's child.* "Whoever acknowledges the Son has the Father also" - 1 John 2:23b NIV.**

Say, "Jesus, I ask You to come into my heart and fill me with Your Spirit so that I can become all You created me to be. Thank You for forgiving me, securing my position as a child of God and giving me eternal life with You and a better life now."

5 Omartian, pgs. 32-33

What have we been saved from? Sin, death, and the devil.

Saved from sin: Everyone since Adam has been born with the inheritance of original sin.

"But I was born a sinner, yes, from the moment my mother conceived me." Psalm 51:5 TLB. Original sin by itself separates us from God. We all commit sins in thoughts, desires, words, and deeds.

Saved from death: *"For the wages of sin is death, but the gift of God is eternal life in Christ Jesus our Lord" - Romans 6:23 NIV.* Billy Graham often said this.

Saved from the devil: *"Be alert and of sober mind. Your enemy the devil prowls around like a roaring lion looking for someone to devour" 1 Peter 5:8 NIV.*

Perhaps Peter remembered his own difficulty in keeping awake during our Lord's agony in Gethsemane. Christ has conquered the devil for us. *"The reason the Son of God appeared was to destroy the devil's work" 1 John 3:8b.*

So whatever your religious background; whatever your long-held beliefs or your deeply cherished sins; whatever it may cost you that Jesus is the new King in town – Paul writes these words for you as the only way you can be saved: *"If you confess with your mouth, '<u>Jesus is Lord</u>,' and believe in your heart that God raised him from the dead, you will be saved." See Romans 10:9 – ESV.*

1- Phil Moore, Straight to the Heart of Romans, Monarch Books, 2014, pg. 175.

"For it is with your heart that you believe and are justified, and it is with your mouth that you confess and are saved" - Romans 10:10 NIV.

As the Scripture says, "Anyone who trusts in him will never be put to shame." For there is no difference between Jew and Gentile – the same Lord is Lord of all and richly blesses all who call on him, for, *"Everyone who calls on the name of the Lord will be saved" - Romans 10:11-13 NIV.*

There is no other way anyone can be saved! *"For by grace you have been saved through faith. And this is not your own doing; it is the gift of God, not a result of works, so that no one may boast" - Ephesians 2:8-9 ESV.*

"If we do something wrong <u>after</u> we receive Jesus, He gives us a way out of that condemnation through <u>confession</u> of the wrong deed and through <u>repentance</u>. Repentance means we decide to turn away from wrong doing and never do it again."

6- Omartian, pg. 29

At times, we may not feel forgiven. Forgiveness does not depend on feeling; it depends on God's promise in His Word.

I'm sure we can all think of a time when we came face-to-face with the depth of our sin and asked ourselves a haunting question. "How could I do that?" I'm a Christian!" Paul tells us not to be surprised to find that we sin after being saved. For although we have been justified by Christ, once for all time, we do not become sinless before we reach heaven. The process of being made holy in sanctification is a road that we travel our entire lives. We will stumble along the way. But no matter the incredible depth of what we have wrongly done, there is an even more incredible depth of forgiveness given by God in Christ to cover us.

The Bible says, *"There is now no condemnation for those who are in Christ Jesus" - Romans 8:1 NIV.*

"He is the only one who can give you life before death as well as after."
7 -Omartian, pg. 30

Jesus is for all people. Jesus loves all people. And all people need Jesus and His salvation.

"Because of Jesus, you can enjoy greater abundance in your life. Jesus said, "I have come that they may have life, and that they may have it abundantly" - John 10:10 ESV. Again, having abundance doesn't mean we will be rich, famous, and accomplished. It means He will give us more than we need."
8-Omartian, pg. 31

Chapter 20

"And I will ask the Father, and he will give you another Helper, to be with you forever." - John 14:16 ESV

The Three in One

The one thing that I never truly understood was about the Trinity. God, Jesus Christ, and the Holy Spirit. It finally clicked one time when I was working on a sermon.

The explanation is very concise but still beyond our full human comprehension. Our God has graciously revealed Himself to us as three distinct persons as God the Father, The Son of God, and the Holy Spirit. Our Lord does not ask us to understand fully the nature of the Trinity, only to believe in the Trinity through the power of the Holy Spirit. His great love for us sent us His Son to suffer and die on the cross for our sake. Through Jesus' death and resurrection from the dead, and through our faith in Him, we are forgiven our sins and saved from eternal separation from God. The Holy Spirit brings us to faith and keeps us in the one true faith unto life everlasting.

"If you learn virtue and goodness only from men or books, you will be virtuous according to time and place and outward forms. You may do works of humility and love. But the inward virtues are only to be obtained by the operation of the Holy Spirit --not outwardly teaching but inwardly bringing forth a newborn spirit within us."
2-Murray, August 11 Reading

Jesus Promises the Holy Spirit - *"If you love me, keep my commands. And I will ask the Father, and he will give you another advocate to help you and be with you forever --- the Spirit of truth. The world cannot accept him, because it neither sees him nor knows him. But you know him, for he lives with you and will be in you. I will not leave you as orphans; I will come to you. Before long, the world will not see me anymore, but you will see me. Because I live, you also will live. On that day you will realize that I am in my Father, and you are in me, and I am in you" - John 14:15-20 NIV.*

"Do you not know that your body is a temple of the Holy Spirit, who is in you, whom you have received from God? You are not your own, you were bought at a price. Therefore honor God with your body" - 1 Cor. 6:19-20 NIV.

Notes- Your body is therefore sacred and is to be treated as sacred (holy), Christians should also realize that by the Spirit's presence and power, they can be helped against things not pleasing to the

Lord.
1-NIV Bible, pg. 2367 (footnotes-1 Cor 6:19)

"I could not live without the presence of the Holy Spirit in my life. When receiving Jesus, the most precious gift you receive is the Holy Spirit. The Holy spirit dwells in every believer."
9-Omartian, pg. 37

"If Christ is in you, then the Holy Spirit is in you as well, and that means you do not have to live in the flesh anymore."
10-Omartian, pgs. 38.

When you receive Jesus, from then on God sees the righteousness of Jesus in you. He sends the Holy Spirit to live in you, and now you can be close to God. You can speak to Him and hear Him speak to your heart. The Holy Spirit helps you to pray, and God hears and answers, not because of what you deserve, but because of what Jesus did. It's called grace.
11-Omartian, pgs. 64-65.

Chapter 21

"Truly I tell you, whatever you bind on earth will be bound in heaven, and whatever you loose on earth will be loosed in heaven." - Matthew 18:18 NIV

Heaven Bound

"But about that day and hour no one knows, not even the angels of heaven, nor the Son, but the Father only" - Matthew 24:36 NIV.

Life isn't easy sometimes. Sometimes our life is full of worry and anguish. Too many days are taken up with heartache and suffering but good news is always uplifting. It feels good to share an exciting story of someone's recovery from an illness or someone rescued from danger. Life even at its best, can't compare to how great heaven is going to be.

"But in keeping with his promise we are looking forward to a new heaven and a new earth, where righteousness dwells" - 2 Peter 3:13 NIV.

"For we know that if the earthly tent we live in is destroyed, we have a building from God, an eternal house in heaven, not built by human hands. Meanwhile we groan, longing to be clothed instead with our heavenly dwelling, because when we are clothed we will not be naked. For while we are in this tent, we groan and are burdened, because we do not wish to be unclothed but to be clothed instead with our heavenly dwelling, so that what is mortal may be swallowed up by life. Now the one who has fashioned us for this very purpose is God, who has given us the Spirit as a deposit, guaranteeing what is to come" - 2 Corinthians 5:1-5 NIV.

"He was afraid and said, 'How awesome is this place! This is none other than the house of God; this is the gate of heaven'" - Genesis 28:17 NIV.

Chapter 22

"Blessed are you when people insult you, persecute you and falsely say all kinds of evil against you because of me" - Matthew 5:11 NIV.

The Beatitudes

Why did I want to include The Beatitudes?

For one, it is Jesus talking in the Sermon on the Mount. He gave these eight blessings in the Gospel of Matthew. Each is a proverb-like proclamation and full of meaning. Our church had a bible study on it a few years ago. So, I am including some spiritual learning that I *was fortunate to receive.*

Matt. 5:3 NIV - "Blessed are the poor in spirit, for theirs is the kingdom of heaven."

Jesus was speaking of spiritual poverty.
One can be financially poor and yet be arrogant and prideful in spirit.
David was the ruler of Israel, yet had a humble spirit.
If you are poor in spirit, you can turn toward God.
When I feel down, I know I can pray to God and he will listen.
P*salm 34:4 NIV- "I sought the Lord, and he answered me; he delivered me from all my fears."*
The kingdom of heaven is not earned but is more a gift than a reward.

Matt. 5:4 NIV - "Blessed are those who mourn, for they will be comforted."

Various reasons for mourning might be:
Loss of a loved one or loss of a job.
Suffering from sickness or disease.
Upset over mistakes or failures.
My life had loss and disappointment. Life wasn't supposed to turn out this way.
In spite of all this, a deep and abiding rest has come into my heart.
What matters most is that love and family matter, peace matters.
Though at times our sinful nature remains in this life, God comforts us with His Word and the Holy Spirit.
My sins were paid for when Christ died and when he comes again, they will be removed from me permanently.

Matt. 5:5 NIV - "Blessed are the meek, for they will inherit the earth."

The meaning of meek – a person with a humble and gentle heart.

It does not mean a weak or subdued person.

It describes a person who is kind and considerate to others.

The inheritance will be the Kingdom of God.

Matt. 5:6 NIV - "Blessed are those who hunger and thirst for righteousness, for they will be filled."

People hunger and thirst for: power, fame, money, beauty and sexuality.

We have daily needs for food and water. Our spirit needs daily food too. Only God can quench our thirst and satisfy our hunger for righteousness.

Righteousness is the way of living right, that comes out of your desire to please God. To hunger and thirst for God, is to desire to know Him more than anything else you want in this world.

Psalm 51:10-12 NIV - "Create in me a pure heart, O God, and renew a steadfast spirit within me. Do not cast me from your presence or take your Holy Spirit from me. Restore to me the joy of your salvation."

Be aware of anything that keeps you from God.

Proverbs 14:16 ESV - "One who is wise is cautious and turns away from evil, but a fool is reckless and careless."

Matt. 5:7 NIV - "Blessed are the merciful, for they will be shown mercy."

Mercy is a special form of love. It sees someone in misery and feels compelled to do something about it.
To be compassionate, helpful, kind, giving towards the weak, sick and poor.
God's mercy moved him to send His Son to save us. Jesus took our sin and guilt upon Himself and suffered God's wrath in our place, that we might be forgiven and inherit eternal life.

Matt. 5:8 NIV - "Blessed are the pure in heart, for they will see God."

How can we be pure? It is beyond our reach to become pure. It is God who initiates, sanctifies and perfects the heart (the center of one's being, including mind, will and emotions) of man who puts his trust in Him.

His promise to the pure in heart is amazing:
"They shall see God." The glories of heaven – a perfect paradise; living in a glorious, perfected body;
delighting in the presence of loved ones and the great saints of old; gazing up the beauty of the angel--nothing will compare to seeing the glorious face of God. Then, our hearts will always be pure, holy, and true.

Matt. 5:9 NIV- "Blessed are the peacemakers, for thy will be called children of God."

The greatest peacemaker is Jesus Christ Himself. His life was perfect, He was innocent, and suffered

and died. Then he was resurrected. He made peace between God and people. Jesus supports peace and encourages the peacemakers.

Jesus said in *Luke 6:27-28 NIV, "Love your enemies, do good to those who hate you, bless those who curse you, pray for those who mistreat you".*

Matt. 5:10 NIV- "Blessed are those who are persecuted because of righteousness, for theirs is the kingdom of heaven".

1 Peter 3:13-15 NIV - "Who is going to harm you if you are eager to do good? But even if you should suffer for what is right, you are blessed. Do not fear their threats; do not be frightened. But in your hearts revere Christ as Lord. Always be prepared to give an answer to everyone who asks you to give the reason for the hope that you have. But do this with gentleness and respect."

Chapter 23

"Be still before the Lord and wait patiently for Him" - Psalm 37:7a NIV.

PRAYER

I must never stop praying for my children and grandchildren as well as those friends with needs and the church members with needs.

"Whenever you feel overwhelmed by what you are carrying, go before God in praise and worship and He will take your burden away."
12-Omartian, pg. 57

"We need to pray, then stop and listen. Sometimes we can

hear God as a still, small voice from deep within our heart.

Many times God will speak in our inner witness so that we "just know" the truth and it sets us free. Suddenly we know what we should do and what we shouldn't do.

King David had a lot to say about seeking God in the morning. He prayed in the morning and then watched and waited for God to speak to his heart. I like knowing that God is listening to our prayers. He likes it when we listen to His answers."

"Let the morning bring me word of your unfailing love, for I have trust in you. Show me the way I should go, for to you I entrust my life" - Psalm 143:8 NIV.
2-Meyer, pg. 14

Before you are fully awake, you can start talking to God. Just thank him for helping you get through yesterday, and for being with you today. Ask him to make you aware of His presence all day long. Peace fills your heart when your mind is on the Lord. Nothing is more satisfying then walking with the Lord.

"But when you pray, go into your room, close the door and pray to your Father, who is unseen" - Matthew 6:6 NIV.

"And when you stand praying, if you hold anything against anyone, forgive them, so that your Father in heaven may forgive you your sins" - Mark 11:25-NIV.

Prayer and God's Word are inseparably linked together. Prayer seeks God; the Word reveals God. In prayer, we ask God; in the Word, God answers us. In prayer, we rise to heaven to dwell with God; in the Word, God comes to dwell with us. In prayer, we give ourselves to God; in the Word, God gives Himself to us.

"And pray in the Spirit on all occasions with all kinds of prayers and requests. With this in mind, be alert and always keep on praying for all the Lord's people" Ephesians 6:18 NIV.

"Jesus is the perfect example of how we are not only to ask that His will be done, but also to leave it entirely in our Father's hands. In the Garden of Gethsemane, Jesus prayed, "My Father, if it be possible, let this cup pass from Me; nevertheless, not as I will, but as You will" - Matthew 26:39 ESV.

This is a wonderful example for us to follow. We are to take our problems and requests to the Lord in prayer and then leave it completely in His hands.

In prayer we intercede for the people and situations around us. In prayer we praise God for all He has done. And we thank Him in advance for all He is doing and will do for us in the future. The more we pray, the more we realize that we cannot live without Him and His power.

Chapter 24

"Do everything in love." - 1 Corinthians 16:14 NIV

Love

I planned my days, Jerry and I planned our years ahead, but things don't always go as we expect. Weather can change, jobs are suddenly terminated, and loved ones pass away. How can we possibly plan with certainty? One thing we can be sure of is our duty while we are here. As the two greatest commandments say, *Love the Lord your God with all your heart and love your neighbor as yourself.* The Bible stands forever. God does not change and neither do His plans for us.

In my first sermon, I was inspired to speak on Love from a

love chapter in Rick Warren's book, The Purpose Driven Life.

My granddaughter, Brianna, who was eight at the time, found out I was doing the sermon instead of Pastor Jamey – she looked at me with those big brown eyes in amazement. I think she was thinking, "Grandma, you've got to be kidding." Then she said, "I'll be so embarrassed." Hopefully she wasn't. I had a message to give.

We Must Love God, each and every one of us. **It is the first and greatest commandment.** In Matthew 22:36-40 NIV, one of the Pharisees asked Jesus,
"Teacher, which is the greatest commandment in the Law? Jesus replied: 'Love the Lord your God with all your heart and with all your soul and with all your mind.' This is the first and greatest commandment. And the second is like it: 'Love your neighbor as yourself.' All the Law and the Prophets hang on these two commandments."

Why should we love God?

1. Because He created us.
2. Because God loves us. He loves us because he has chosen to love us. Personally, powerfully, passionately. He loves me because he has chosen to love me. He loves me when I don't feel like being loved. He loves me when no one else loves me. Others may abandon me, ignore me, but God will always love me, no matter what.
3. Another reason we should love God is because He wants us to love Him. God's plan includes a love relationship between him and humanity.

If you do love Him:

You will be extremely happy.

You'll prosper.
Your prayers will be answered.
You'll enjoy deep peace.
You'll see God's glory.
You'll have power over the devil.

The second greatest commandment is, *"Love your neighbor as yourself"* *Luke 10:27b NIV.*

What about the people you don't care much about? One you might dislike or one you actually cannot get along with. A Christian should love his enemies. That is, he **is** to treat his enemies with proper respect, but he is not commanded to have a warm emotional affection toward them.

"Do not seek revenge or bear a grudge against one of your people, but love your neighbor as yourself. I am the Lord" - Leviticus 19:18 NIV.

"Your strong love for each other will prove to the world that you are my disciples" John 13:35 LB.
2-Murray, February 5 Reading.

Will we ever love perfectly? No. This side of heaven only God will.
Jesus' death on the cross was love at its highest. We owe everything to this love. Love is the power that moved Christ to die for us. In love, God highly exalted Him as Lord and Christ. Love is the power through which Christ dwells and works in us. Love can change my nature and enable me to surrender to God. It gives me strength to live a holy, joyous life, full of blessings to others. Every Christian should show the love of God.

"The love of God is not just a feeling or an emotion, It is the Spirit of God in us. When we receive Jesus, we receive the love of God and nothing can change that."
13-Omartian, pg. 79

If we fully believe that the Holy Spirit, welling within us, will maintain this heavenly love from hour to hour, we will be able to understand the words of Christ: *"Everything is possible for one who believes" - Mark 9:23b NIV.* Then we will be able to love God with all our hearts, to love family and friends, and even our enemies.

I don't want to be important in anyway. I want to be humble. I want to love people. I want to be kind. I want to be like Jesus. I want to do for others as long as I can. God has done so much for me. Jesus died on the cross for me. The Holy Spirit lives in me. How fortunate I have been. I had two of the most lovely parents who loved their children very much.

"Dear friends, let us love one another, for love comes from God. Everyone who loves has been born of God and knows God" - John 4:7 NIV.

Quotes by Known Authors

A quote by Corrie Ten Boom - "You can never learn that Christ is all you need, until Christ is all you have."

The Last Rose of Summer

'Tis the last rose of summer left blooming alone;
All her lovely companions are faded and gone;
No flower of her kindred, no rosebud is nigh,
To reflect back her blushes, and give sign for sigh.

I'll not leave thee, thou lone one, to pine on the stem;
Since the lovely are sleeping,
Go sleep thou with them.
Thus kindly I scatter, thy leaves o'er the bed
Where thy mates of the garden lie scentless and dead.

So soon may I follow, when friendships decay,
And from Love's shining circle the gems drop away.
When true hearts lie withered, and fond ones are flown,
Oh! who would inhabit this bleak world alone?

Author-Thomas Moore, an Irish poet who wrote it in 1805. He was inspired by a specimen of Rosa 'Old Blush'.

Abraham Lincoln said: "I believe the Bible is the best gift God has ever given to man. All the good from The Savior of the world is communicated to us through this Book."

Abraham Lincoln said: "Happiness is a choice."

Abraham Lincoln said: "After a great deal of study of the scriptures, your Christian faith is inspired."

Abraham Lincoln said: "My concern is not whether God is on our side; my greatest concern is to be on God's side, for God is always right."

Abraham Lincoln said: "The better part of one's life consists of his friendships."

Sayings by Unknown Authors

Danish proverb-What you are is God's gift to you; what you do with yourself is your gift to God.

Thank God our righteousness does not depend on ourselves.

God will never forget us. You can't use him up or wear him out. Hang on to him.

If you want your life to work, begin each day by saying, "Thank You, heavenly Father, for this day".

A man who was diagnosed with cancer told everyone he was in a win-win situation: "If I am healed, I get to spend more time on earth with my loved ones. If not, I get to live eternally with Christ." *"Do not withhold your mercy from me, Lord; may your love and faithfulness always protect me" Psalm 40:11 NIV.*

I thank God every day for my blessed life. I'm not rich, don't live in a mansion and don't have the nicest of material things, but I'm fairly healthy, have a roof over my head, clothes on my back, food on my table, a family that loves me and lifelong friends to get me through, I'd say I have a lot to be thankful for.

Some of My Favorite Scriptures

"I can do all things through him who gives me strength" - Phillipians 4:13 NIV.

"And without faith it is impossible to please God, because anyone who comes to him must believe that he exists and that he rewards those who earnestly seek him" Hebrews 11:6 NIV.

"Here is a trustworthy saying:
If we have died with him, we will also live with him;
If we endure, we will also reign with him;
If we deny him, he also will deny us;
If we are faithless, he remains faithful,
for he cannot disown himself" - 2 Timothy 2:11-13 NIV.

This was probably an early Christian hymn. The point to which Paul appeals is that suffering for Christ will be followed by glory. 2-Footnotes from my NIV Bible, pg. 2496.

"Very truly I tell you, whoever hears my word and believes him who has sent me has eternal life and will not be judged but has crossed over from death to life. Very truly I tell you, a time is coming and has now come when the dead will hear the voice of the Son of God and those who hear will live. For as the Father has life in himself, so he has granted the son also to have life in himself. And he has given him authority to judge because he is the Son of Man. Do not be amazed at this, for a time is coming when all who are in their graves will hear his voice and come out – those who have done what is good will rise to live, and those who have done what is evil will rise to be condemned. By myself I can do nothing; I judge only as I hear, and my judgment is just, for I seek not to please myself but him who sent me" John 5:24-30 NIV.

Salvation, of course, is a gift from God in response to faith, but true faith in Christ results in changed lives, lived in obedience to Christ as Lord. ***Footnotes from my NIV Bible, for John 5:29. pg. 2176.***

"Because you have seen me, you have believed; blessed are those who have not seen and yet have believed" John 20:29 NIV.

"For it is by grace you have been saved, through faith – and this is not from yourselves, it is the gift of God – not by works, so that no one can boast "Ephesians 2:8-9 NIV.

God knows exactly how long we'll live and when we'll die. *"You saw me before I was born, and scheduled each day of my life before I began to breathe. Every day was recorded in your book" Psalms 139:16 TLB.*

"Be kind and compassionate to one another, forgiving each other, just as in Christ God forgave you" - Ephesians 4:32 NIV.

"But seek first the kingdom of God and His righteousness, and all these things will be provided for you. Therefore don't worry about tomorrow, because tomorrow will worry about itself. Each day has enough trouble of its own" - Matthew 6:33-34 NIV.

"Be alert and of sober mind. Your enemy, the devil, prowls around like a roaring lion looking for someone to devour. Resist him, standing firm in the faith, because you know that the family of believers throughout the world is undergoing the same kind of sufferings" - 1 Peter 5:8-9 NIV.

Thank You, Father God, that when I need hope, you are my Hope (Psalm 71:5).
When I am weak, Your are my Strength (Isaiah 12:2).
When I am weary, You are my Resting Place (Jeremiah 50:6).
When I need freedom, You are my Deliverer (Psalm 70:5).

When I want guidance, You are my Counselor (Psalm 16:7).
When I need healing, You are my Healer (Malachi 4:2)
When I seek protection, You are my Shield (Psalm 33: 20).
When I am going through a difficult time,
You are my Stronghold in the Day of Trouble (Nahum 1:7).
Thank You for being my heavenly Father and the answer to my every need.

Epilogue
Grandpa Thurber and James Thurber

Grandpa spent most of his last days working on the Thurber genealogy. He wrote many letters all over the United States trying to get information from many families. Grandpa was working to publish his book, on the genealogy of the Thurber family. After he died, mother had a two large trunks of his records.

One time a gentleman from Ohio State University came and spent a couple of weeks going over grandpa's records. The gentleman was looking for any records that had to do with James Thurber. Grandpa said we were related to James Thurber.

I have confirmed this from the Thurber Genealogy. Charles Henry Thurber, Sr. and James Grover Thurber were 9th generation Thurbers and were descended from James Thurber, son of John and Priscilla Thurber (the "first Thurber's").

James Grover Thurber was an American cartoonist, author, journalist, playwright, and celebrated wit. He was thought of the greatest American humorist since Mark Twain.

He loved dogs of all sizes. He included dogs in many of his drawings. He said "*Dogs represent balance, serenity, and is a sound creature in a crazy world.*"

He was born in Columbus, Ohio. His father, Charles L. Thurber, was a clerk and minor politician. His mother Mary, was a strong-minded woman and a practical joker. Thurber described her as "a born comedienne" and "one of the finest comic talents he'd ever known." One of his books was about his family, My Life and Hard Times (made into a film, *Rise and Shine*).

From 1913 to 1918, Thurber attended Ohio State University. He struggled with some courses partly because of his poor eyesight. He was shot in the eye while playing a bow-and-arrow game, William Tell, with his brother when he was seven. It caused blindness in one eye and it was replaced with a glass eye. The sight in his other eye continued to fail throughout his adult life. He left the university in 1918 without completing his degree.

In 1922, he married Althea Adams. They had one daughter, Rosemary. The marriage was unhappy and ended in divorce.

In 1925 he was in Paris writing for the *Chicago Tribune.*

In 1926 he moved to New York City. Was a reporter at the *Evening Post.*

Later he was at the *The New Yorker*. His cartoons were on the covers of the *New Yorker.* He left *The New Yorker* staff in 1933, but remained still its contributor.

Other works: *The Male Animal* -was a play and film starring Henry Fonda and Olivia De Havilland. Musical version in 1952 starred Ronald Reagan and Virginia Mayo.

My World and Welcome to It - includes the story, *The Secret Life of Walter Mitty.* Filmed in 1947 with Danny Kaye, Virginia Mayo, and Boris Karloff. Filmed in 2013, directed by and starring Ben Stiller.

His second wife, Helen, helped him with his writings.

His eyesight became worse in the 1940's and by the 1950s his blindness was nearly total. He continued to compose stories in his head, and he played himself in 88 performances of the play, *A Thurber Carnival* (1945).

In later years he suffered from alcoholism and depression, but Helen's devoted nursing enabled him to maintain his literary production. One of his drinking friends was Humphrey Bogart.

My mother use to tell about hearing from Helen even after his death in 1961 from a blood clot on the brain.

In 1994, there was a US Postal stamp of him on the 100th anniversary of his birth.

He received posthumously his Doctorate from Ohio State University. His daughter, Rosemary, accepted this in 1995.

The Thurber House in Columbus, Ohio was opened as a literary arts center and museum of Thurber materials. It was the home of James Thurber and his family and is listed on the National Registry of Historic Places. It is a living museum open to the public daily.

A family from California came to mothers and she gave them the records and the Thurber Book of genealogy was published.

A later writer, Joseph Heller, was influenced by James Thurber's stories. That name popped out to me because he had Guillain-Barre' Syndrome. He wrote a book about his illness and difficulties with Speed Vogel named, *No Laughing Matter*. One of his famous books was *Catch 22*, which was made into a movie.

Guillain-Barre' Sydrome Foundation

I have remained connected to the Guillain-Barre' Syndrome Foundation for 20 years because I continue to be inspired by its mission of sharing, caring, and fostering research that will, hopefully, one day lead to a cure. I continue to receive their magazine, The Communicator. It keeps me updated on the upcoming meetings, conventions, and stories of others who have gone through similar situations. It also has articles on research and studies of GBS and CIDP. It is now called GBS/CIDP Foundation International. The international office is:

GBS/CIDP Foundation International
International Office
The Holly Building
104 ½ Forrest Ave. Narbert, PA 19072
www.gbs-cidp.org.
National office 610-667-0131

Our Grandchildren

A few words about our grandchildren:
Daniel Jay Miller (DJ) 1st grandson. Born 1989. Son of Mark and Renee Miller. Graduated from Central Montcalm Schools, Stanton, MI. Adventuresome. Loves to parachute from airplanes, climb mountains, camp in the woods. Worked on the Appalachian Trail in Maine. Qualified in rescuing. Worked as a rapid river rafting guide in Tennessee in the summer 2015. Attended First Congregational Church. Baptized in Clifford Lake. Member of the Michigan Lodge of Free and Accepted Masons, Trufant, MI

Carlton Miller - 2nd grandson. Born 1990. Son of Scott and Barb Miller. Attended Greenville Schools, Central Montcalm, and graduated from Bear Lake Schools. Graduated with B.S. HVAC/R Engineering Technology at Ferris State University. He is a Systems Engineer for a new company, CBRE in Brookfield, WI.
The company controls heating, air conditioning, and lighting

systems for large retail stores nationwide. The clients that he works on mostly are Kohls, Cabelas, and Gander Mountains.
At one point he stated, "I look back at everything that has happened and realize that it happens for a reason. God has a plan for everyone and I'm just trying to make the best of it. I am happy and can't wait to see where my life takes me."

Brandon Miller - 3rd grandson. Born 1993. Son of Scott and Barbara Miller. Attended Greenville Public School, Bear Lake Schools, and graduated from Frankfort Schools. Graduated with B.S. in Accounting in 2016 from Concordia Lutheran University, Ann Arbor, Michigan.

Serena Miller- 1st granddaughter. Born in 1995. Daughter of Mark and Renee Miller. Attended Central Montcalm Schools, Kenawa Hills Schools, and graduated from Cedar Springs Schools. She has been attending Grand Valley State University for pre-medical.

Brianna Miller - 2nd granddaughter. Born in 1997. Daughter of Scott and Barbara Miller. Attended Bear Lake Schools and graduated from Frankfort Schools. Attending Northwestern Michigan College. Plans on entering pre-pharmacy program at Ferris State University this fall.

Katlin Nalett- 3rd granddaughter. Born in 1998. Daughter of Joseph and Angela Nalett. Attended Central Montcalm Schools and plans to graduate this year from Charlotte Public Schools. Plans to go to Lansing Community College for accounting.

My family from days gone by

Family Reunion 2015

Recipes

Curry Chicken

½ bag of chicken frozen pieces (cooked)
Bag of California blend vegetables
1 can cream of chicken soup
1 cup mayonnaise (not Miracle Whip)
Dash lemon juice
½ tsp. curry powder
Mix.
Stir above ingredients.
Pour into greased 9 x 13" baking dish
Bake 1 hour @ 350 degrees.
Top with tater tots, bread crumbs, or Panko
Parmesan cheese
Seasoning if desired
Drizzle of melted butter

Bake 350 degrees 1 hour

Apple-Butternut Bisque-Soup

¼ cup margarine
1 cup coarsely chopped onion
2 cups chopped peeled apples
4 cups cubed peeled butternut squash
1 cup chopped celery
1 tablespoon molasses
2 tablespoons honey
2 teaspoons salt
¼ teaspoon pepper
¼ nutmeg
1/2 cup whipping cream
4 cups chicken stock

Heat margarine in large heavy saucepan until foamy. Add onion. Sauté until tender. Add apples, squash, celery, and chicken stock.
Simmer covered, for 15-20 minutes or until squash is tender. Let stand until cool. Puree in blender or food processor; return to saucepan. Bring to a simmer. Stir in molasses, honey, salt, pepper, nutmeg, and ½ cup cream. Heat to serving temperature. Freezes well.

Broccoli-Cauliflower Cheese Soup

From cousin, Deb Wisman
May 2008

1 lg. Broccoli bunch
1 med head cauliflower
2 carrots
4 cups water
3 chicken bouillon cubes
4 Tbl. oleo
4 Tbl. flour
1 can of Cream of
Chicken Soup

In large pot-boil veggies in water with above ingredients until tender. (About 20 min.)
In another sauce pan- 4 slices of American cheese
1 tsp. salt
½ t. pepper
1-12 oz. can evaporated milk, oleo and water.
Blend over low heat until blended & melted.
Mash veggies in water, add cheese mixture & simmer.

Pork Chop with Potatoes & Tomatoes Casserole

This recipe was Grandma Nielsen's. She found it in a Sunday paper.

4- 6 pork chops
Approx 10 potatoes- peeled & sliced
1 medium to large onion- sliced

Stewed tomatoes -2 large cans
Salt & pepper to taste

Parboil potatoes slices and onions slices until you can puncture with a fork.
Drain liquid. Pour into casserole dish. Cover with stewed tomatoes. Add uncooked pork chops to top of mixture. Salt & pepper. Cover pork chops with stewed tomatoes. Salt & pepper. Bake uncovered at 350 degrees for 1 ½ hours. Leftovers are good for the next day.

Bibliography

Omartian, Stormie – The Power of a Praying Life, Harvest House Publishers, 2010.

Meyer, Joyce – Starting Your Day Right, Devotions for Each Morning of the Year, Faith Works, 2003.

Moore, Phil - Straight to the Heart of Romans, Monarch Books, 2014.

Murray, Andrew -Teach Me to Pray, Daily Devotional Insights, Barbour Publishing, 2004.

New International Bible, Zondervan, 2002.

The Communicator, GBS/CIDP Foundation International magazine, Spring 2013.

Made in the USA
Monee, IL
12 February 2021

60395677R00079